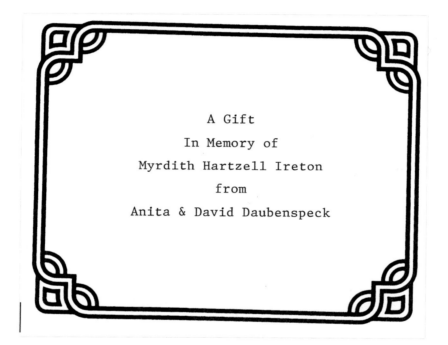

A Gift
In Memory of
Myrdith Hartzell Ireton
from
Anita & David Daubenspeck

What is it made of?

Dorling  Kindersley

LONDON, NEW YORK, SYDNEY, DELHI, PARIS, MUNICH, and JOHANNESBURG

Project Editors: Judith Hodge, Angela Wilkes, Sue Malyan, Carey Scott
Project Art Editors: Michelle Baxter, Rebecca Johns, Emy Manby
Senior Editor: Sarah Levete
Editors: Dawn Rowley, Anna Lofthouse
Senior Art Editors: Chris Scollen, Adrienne Hutchinson
Managing Editors: Linda Martin, Mary Atkinson
Managing Art Editor: Peter Bailey
Senior DTP Designer: Bridget Roseberry
Production: Erica Rosen
Picture Researchers: Louise Thomas, Marie Osborn
Computer-generated artwork: Alternative View
Photography: Steve Gorton, Gary Ombler
Jacket Designers: Karen Burgess, Sophia Tampakopoulos

First American Edition, 2001
00 01 02 03 04 05 10 9 8 7 6 5 4 3 2 1

Published in the United States by Dorling Kindersley Publishing, Inc.
95 Madison Avenue, New York, New York 10016

Copyright © 2001 Dorling Kindersley Limited
A Pearson Company

A Cataloging-in-Publication record is available from the Library of Congress

ISBN 0-7894-1251-7

Color reproduction by Colourscan, Singapore
Printed and bound in Italy by L.E.G.O.

The publisher would like to thank the following for their kind permission to reproduce their photographs:
a=above; c=center; b=below; l=left; r=right; t=top

Bruce Coleman Ltd: C. B. & D. W. Frith 17cr; **Bruce Coleman Ltd:** Kim Taylor 33t; **Bubbles:** Jennie Woodcock 27tl; **Corbis UK Ltd:** Anthony Cooper 17t; **Gables:** 17cr; **Gettyone Stone:**
Charles Thatcher 31tr; **Robert Harding Picture Library:** J. Lightfoot 15t; Mark Mawson 23b; **Robert Harding Picture Library:** 19tl; M. Chillmaid 29tl; **Image Bank:** Elyse Lewin 17tl; **Image Bank:** Andrea Pistolesi 21t; **Image Bank:** Ross Whitaker 27br; **Images Colour Library:** 21tr; **Pictor International:** 23tl, 25tl; **Brian Pitkin** 31t; **Powerstock Photolibrary/Zefa:** Monica Wells 15tl; **Rex Features:** 29tl; **Science**
Photo Library: Jeremy Walker 33tl; **Telegraph Colour Library:** Bavaria – Bildagentur 19t; Bluestone Productions 28b; **Telegraph Colour Library:** Colorific 27tl; Eduardo Garcia 19tl; J. Cummins 21tr; **Telegraph Colour Library:** 31tl.

see our complete catalog at **www.dk.com**

Experiments in Science

What is it made of?

written by David Glover

DK

A Dorling Kindersley Book

Contents

Testing Materials

25.00

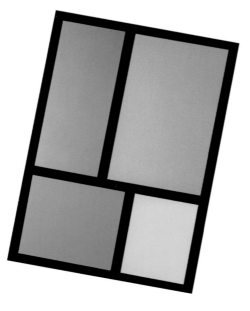

Using Materials

Changing Materials

Wonderful Water

Hello!

Meet Chip, Pixel, and their helpful dog, Newton. Join these three friendly characters as they take you on an exciting and fact-filled journey of scientific discovery.

I'm Chip!

I'm Pixel!

Grrrr, I'm Newton!

Before you begin

You'll need an adult to help you with the experiments in this book. Before starting, read the introduction, the list of equipment, and the instructions. Make sure you look at the numbers on the instructions – they'll help you follow the steps one by one.

After reading the instructions, try to work out what you think will happen. After the experiment, think back to what you predicted. Did it happen as you expected?

Your scientific equipment

Look for the box like this by each experiment. Inside, you'll find a list of all the equipment you'll need – but remember to ask an adult before you use anything.

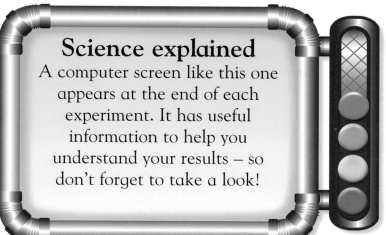

Science explained

A computer screen like this one appears at the end of each experiment. It has useful information to help you understand your results – so don't forget to take a look!

Science in real life

For each experiment, there's a photo showing a real-life example of the science that you're investigating. Can you think of any more real-life examples?

Extra information

At the back of the book, you'll find a glossary that tells you the meanings of new words. There's also an index to help you find your way around the book.

For your helper

Each section of this book has parents' notes especially for the adult who's helping you. The parents' notes for Testing Materials are on pages 16–17, for Using Materials on pages 42–43, for Changing Materials on pages 68–69, and for Wonderful Water on pages 94–95.

Get experimenting and have fun!

Test your knowledge

When you've finished all the experiments in each section, find out how much you remember by doing the fun quiz at the end.

Science safety

Science experiments are fun, but you still need to be careful. Read through the instructions with an adult to see where you might need help.

Be especially careful when using any sharp tools, such as scissors. Always use round-ended scissors and, if necessary, ask an adult to help you.

Whenever you see this symbol, you should be extra careful and always ask an adult for help.

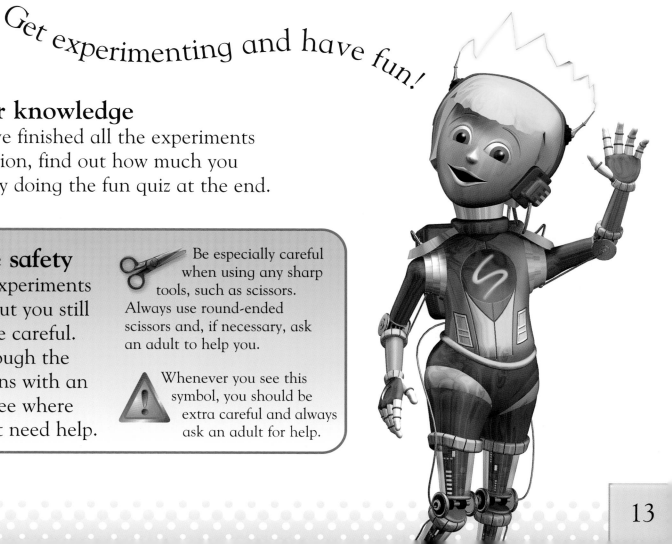

13

Testing Materials

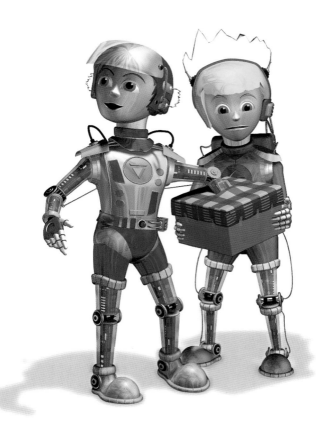

Parents' notes

This section will help your child to develop an understanding of materials and their properties. He or she will discover how to test different materials. Read these notes and any on the relevant pages to help your child get the most out of the experiments.

Pages 18–19: Feeling materials

Here your child is encouraged to feel familiar objects – his or her favorite toys. This activity helps your child recognize that objects made of the same material often feel the same; for example, many plastics are smooth and light.

Pages 20–21: Shiny and dull

The activity on these pages encourages your child to distinguish between shiny and dull objects, first by collecting a variety of different objects and then by sorting them. You might like to explain that smooth materials are often shiny because they reflect a lot of light, and rougher materials are duller because they do not reflect as much light.

Pages 22–23: Is it see-through?

Here your child discovers that some materials are see-through, or transparent, others let some light pass through, while some block out all light. Supervise the length of time your child holds each material over the flashlight. Warn your child never to cover other light sources, such as a naked flame or a lamp, with any material, since this could cause a fire.

Pages 24–25: How hard?

The property of hardness can be tested using a simple scratch test. Explain that if one object can scratch another object, the object that scratches is harder than the object that is scratched.

Pages 26–27: How strong?

In this experiment, your child will test the strength of objects made from different materials. If necessary, shorten one or more of the items until they are all the same length. This will help to create a fair test. Make sure your child holds each piece away from his or her face.

Pages 28–29: Float or sink?

In the first part of this activity, your child will discover that a material floats or sinks depending on whether it seems light or heavy. The activity then introduces the idea of density, which is a measure of how heavy something is in relation to its size. An object floats if it is less dense than water. Reshaping the ball of modeling clay into a boat shape spreads the weight out over a larger area. The clay boat floats because it is larger, and therefore less dense, than a solid ball of clay of the same weight.

Pages 30–31: Mop it up!

Make sure that your child does this experiment on a tray and is wearing some protective clothing. To make the test fair, help your child to measure the same amount of water into the pitcher each time and to cut the materials to a similar size. The sponge is the best material for soaking up liquid because it is thick and full of air holes, which hold the water.

Pages 32–33: Is it waterproof?

Your child should wear protective clothing for this experiment. He or she will learn that the most waterproof material is plastic because it has no holes through which water can pass.

Pages 34–35: Which is warm?

Do not pour boiling hot water into the cups since your child will be using his or her fingers to test the results. Encourage your child to look at winter and summer clothes and to describe and compare the materials. This will help him or her predict the results of the activity.

Pages 36–37: Amazing magnets

Here your child will learn that a steel or iron object, such as a paper clip, is attracted to a magnet, but a nonmetallic object, such as a matchstick, is not. Some metals, for example aluminum, are also not magnetic.

Feeling materials

Do you know what material your favorite toy is made from? What does the toy feel like? Is it soft, heavy or light, rough or smooth? Is it made out of cloth, wood, plastic, or metal? Can you describe the feel of different materials to a friend?

Now play this game
You will need: ★ a cardboard box ★ 2 pieces of cloth or card ★ scissors ★ objects made of different materials, such as metal, plastic, wood, and stone ★ adhesive tape ★ a friend to play with

metal spoon

cork

glass marble

stone

1 Put all the objects into the box.

Be careful when using scissors.

2 Cover half the box with one piece of cloth. Tape the cloth in place.

Playing with materials

At home and outside, you can feel lots of different materials. By the seaside, the sand feels rough and gritty. Plastic buckets and balls feel smooth and cool to touch.

This feels heavy...

Make sure you can't see the objects through the gap.

3 Cover and tape the other half of the box with the other piece of cloth. Put your hand through the gap and feel one of the objects in the box.

4 Tell your friend what the object feels like. Can your friend guess what the object is?

Shiny and dull

A brand-new bicycle is bright and shiny. The smooth metal parts sparkle in the sunshine. The plastic in the lamp is shiny, too. But not all the parts are so bright. The black rubber tires and the leather saddle look dull.

Now make a poster
You will need: ★ a large sheet of paper ★ a ruler ★ a pen ★ nontoxic glue ★ different objects, such as paper clips, buttons, corks, marbles, candy wrappers, leaves, twigs, beads, candy, matchsticks, nuts, wood shavings, and dried pasta

1 Make a poster like this, with the headings "Dull" and "Shiny."

2 Put all the objects together. Then try to sort them into two piles, one of shiny objects and the other of dull objects.

Dull

Shiny

Use a ruler to draw two columns.

Look carefully to see if an object is shiny or dull.

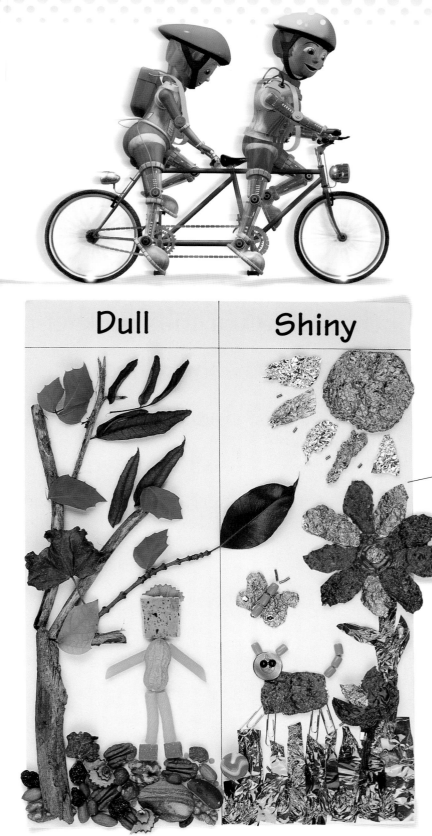

A shiny nest

Bower birds like shiny objects, such as brightly colored berries, buttons, and glass beads. Can you spot the bower bird hiding in the nest behind the berries?

When the glue is dry, you can put the poster on your wall.

Dull	Shiny

Science explained

The shiny objects are made from smooth materials, such as metal or glass. They shine because they reflect light, like a mirror. If you polish a shiny object, it will shine more brightly. The dull objects have rougher surfaces that don't sparkle in the light.

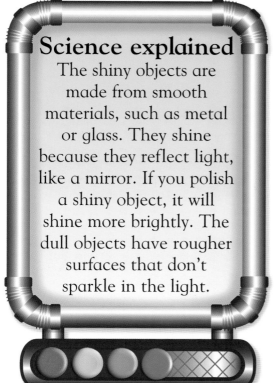

3 Put the dull objects on one side of the poster and the shiny objects on the other side. Try to make a picture with your objects, and then glue them in place.

Is it see-through?

You can see through a glass window because it's clear. It lets lots of light pass through. Thin curtains block some light, but you can still see light through them. Bricks block all the light that falls on them, so you can't see through a brick wall!

Now try this experiment

You will need: ★ a pen ★ a sheet of paper ★ a ruler ★ a flashlight ★ a rubber band ★ materials to test, such as a glass, thick cardboard, plastic wrap, colored paper, aluminum foil, and a dishcloth.

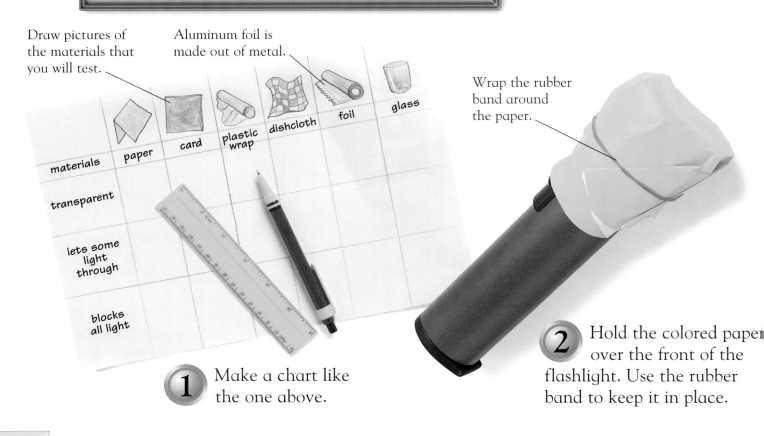

Draw pictures of the materials that you will test.

Aluminum foil is made out of metal.

Wrap the rubber band around the paper.

1 Make a chart like the one above.

2 Hold the colored paper over the front of the flashlight. Use the rubber band to keep it in place.

Science explained

Glass and plastic wrap are completely see-through, or transparent. A dishcloth or thin, colored material, such as paper, let some light through. You could block out more light with lots of layers of these materials. Metals and thick layers of materials block out all the light.

See-through houses

Sheds or houses made of glass, like this huge greenhouse, are used for growing plants. Sunlight passes easily through the see-through panes of glass. This gives seeds and plants the light and warmth they need to grow, but keeps out cold winds.

⚠ Never cover other light sources with materials – they could burn.

3 Turn on the flashlight. Does the paper let all the light through, just some, or none? Turn off the flashlight. Record your results on the chart.

Keep the flashlight on for a short time only, otherwise the paper will get too hot.

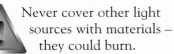

Hold the glass over the light from the flashlight.

4 Now try shining the flashlight through the glass, and then through the other materials. Fill in your results on the chart.

23

How hard?

Some materials are hard and some are soft. It is easy to scratch a soft material, like soap, but it's difficult to scratch a hard material, like metal. Which do you think is harder – wood or stone? Try this test to find out.

Now try this scratching test
You will need: ★ a used matchstick ★ a wax candle ★ a piece of cardboard ★ a metal coin ★ a stone

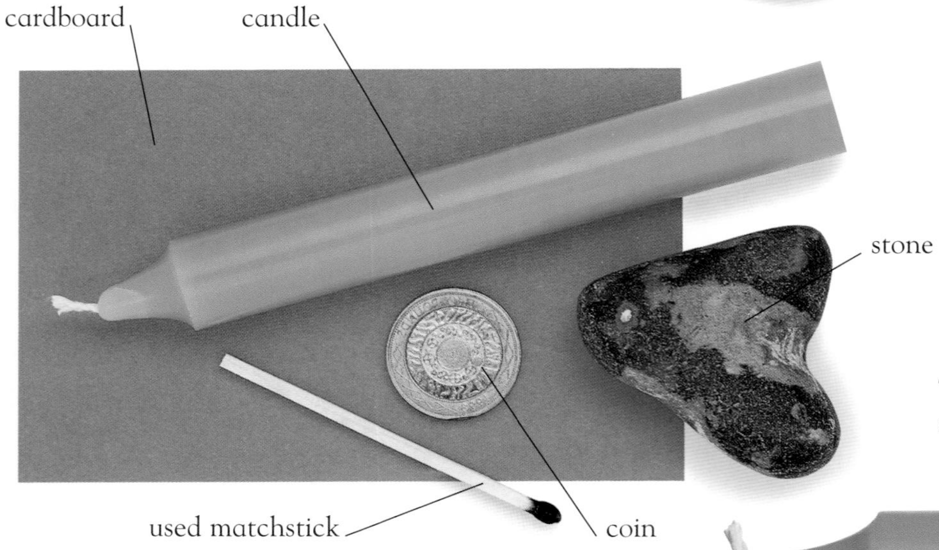

cardboard

candle

stone

used matchstick

coin

1 Collect all your materials. The matchstick is your wooden scratcher.

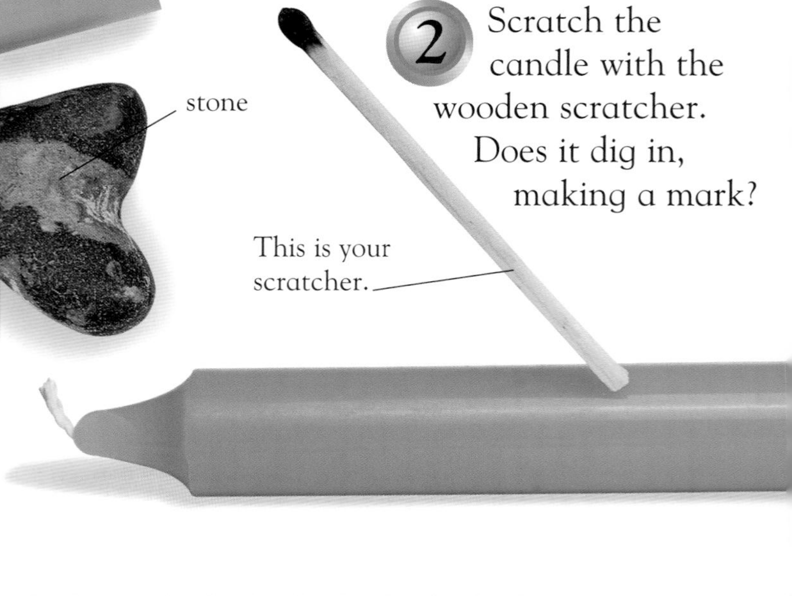

2 Scratch the candle with the wooden scratcher. Does it dig in, making a mark?

This is your scratcher.

A real diamond

Diamond is the hardest material of all. A real diamond, like this one, will scratch stone, metal, and glass, but a fake diamond won't make a mark on these materials.

3 Now try to scratch the stone, the cardboard, and the coin. Does the scratcher mark all these materials?

4 Try using each of the other materials as the scratcher, like Newton is doing. What happens?

How strong?

Have you ever seen a road bridge made out of glass? Of course not! It would break with the weight of the traffic crossing it. Strong bridges are made from metal, stone, or concrete. These materials can carry the huge weight of cars and trucks. Strong things do not break easily.

Now try this strength test
You will need: ★ a sheet of paper ★ a pen ★ a ruler ★ a large, metal paper clip ★ dry spaghetti ★ a plastic toothpick ★ a wooden toothpick

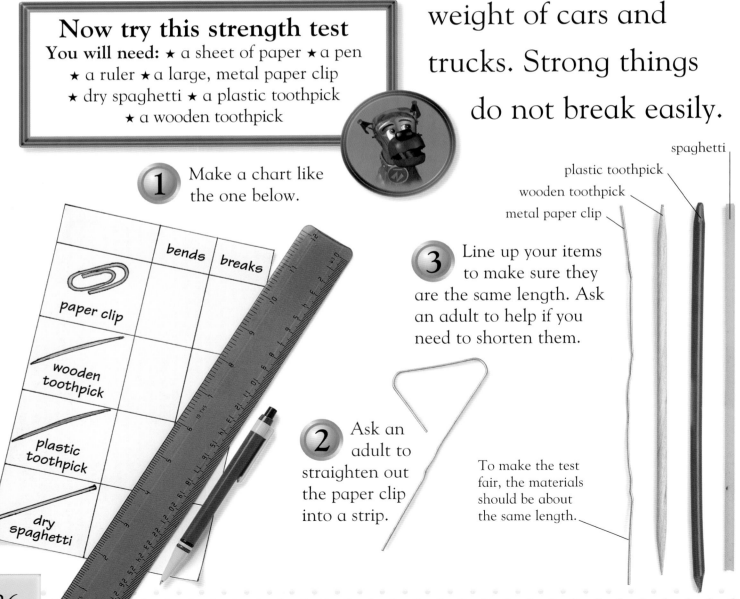

1 Make a chart like the one below.

3 Line up your items to make sure they are the same length. Ask an adult to help if you need to shorten them.

2 Ask an adult to straighten out the paper clip into a strip.

To make the test fair, the materials should be about the same length.

spaghetti
plastic toothpick
wooden toothpick
metal paper clip

	bends	breaks
paper clip		
wooden toothpick		
plastic toothpick		
dry spaghetti		

Suspension bridge

This huge suspension bridge is made from concrete and metal. Thick metal wires support the weight of the road, trucks, and cars.

4 Carefully hold the straightened paper clip at either end. Bend it slowly. Is it difficult to bend? Does it break?

⚠ When you bend the items, hold them away from your face.

5 Now test each of the other materials. Fill in the results on your chart.

Science explained

Metal is easier to bend than wood, but it is harder to break. Plastic bends easily, but may snap if you bend it too far. Spaghetti snaps easily. This means that metal is the strongest material and spaghetti is the weakest material.

27

Float or sink?

If you throw a stone in a pond, it will sink to the bottom. Solid heavy materials usually sink, and light materials usually float. Try this experiment to see how to make heavy materials float.

Now try this test

You will need: ★ a metal spoon ★ a ball of modeling clay ★ a plastic spoon ★ a cork ★ a pebble ★ a bowl of water

1 Hold each object to feel how much it weighs. Carefully put the objects into the bowl of water. What happens?

metal spoon

ball of modeling clay

Push your thumb into the middle of the clay.

2 Take the objects out of the bowl. Now push your thumb into the modeling clay to make a boat shape.

cork

plastic spoon

pebble

Huge ships

This huge ship is carrying heavy containers full of goods. The ship can float on the water because its hollow shape makes it light for its huge size.

3 Now put the boat shape in the water. Does it float or sink?

Gently lower the boat shape into the water.

Science explained

Some materials are heavier than others. Things made from solid metal or stone usually sink. But most solid wood, cork, or plastic things float. A ball of heavy modeling clay sinks. But you can make it float by shaping it into a hollow boat. It now floats because it is lighter for its size.

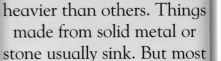

Mop it up!

Have you ever spilled a drink? You need something to mop up the mess. Some materials are good at soaking up water. The water fills tiny holes in the material. But which is the best material for mopping up? Is it sponge, cloth, or paper?

Now try this test

You will need: ★ a measuring pitcher half-full of water ★ a plastic container ★ a sponge ★ a spoon ★ 3 plastic cups ★ a sheet of paper towel ★ a dishcloth ★ a friend to help

1 Pour half a pitcher of water into the plastic container.

Hold the sponge down with the spoon.

2 Put the sponge in the container. Push it under the water and count slowly to 20.

sponge

3 Squeeze the water out of the sponge into one of the cups.

Squeeze as much water as you can out of the sponge.

Half fill the pitcher with water for each test.

container   spoon

4 Repeat the test with the paper towel and then with the dishcloth. Always start with half a pitcher of water in the container.

Squeeze water from the paper towel and the dishcloth into separate empty cups.

paper towel

dishcloth

5 Look at the amounts of water in the cups. Which material soaked up most water?

Science explained

The sponge, paper towel, and dishcloth are good at soaking up water because they are full of tiny holes. The more holes there are in a material, the more water it can hold. The sponge has most space inside its holes, so it probably soaked up most water.

Soapy sponges

Have you ever helped to wash a car? You use a sponge soaked in water and soap to wash away the dirt.

Is it waterproof?

Have you ever been caught in the rain without a raincoat? The rain goes straight through your clothes! Most clothes are not waterproof. Raincoats and rubber boots keep you cozy and dry because they are made from materials that water cannot pass through.

Now test these materials

You will need: ★ a bowl ★ a piece of plastic ★ a large rubber band ★ a pitcher of water ★ 2 old, cotton handkerchiefs or cloths ★ a wax crayon

1 Cover the bowl with the plastic. Hold it in place with the rubber band.

2 Pour some water onto the plastic. Does the water go through into the bowl?

Watch what happens to the water.

Put the bowl in a sink.

Be careful when putting the rubber band on the bowl.

Rainy day

Splish, splash! If you wear waterproof clothes or hold an umbrella, you can play in the rain without getting too wet. These things are made from materials that water can't pass through.

Science explained

There are lots of tiny holes between the threads of a cotton hanky. Water can pass through these holes. Rubbing the hanky with a wax crayon fills the holes with wax and stops the water from getting through. Plastic doesn't have any holes so it is completely waterproof.

3 Test one of the hankies in the same way. Is it waterproof?

Put the rubber band around the hanky.

4 Now rub the other hanky all over with the wax crayon. Repeat the test with this hanky. Is it more or less waterproof than the other hanky?

Make sure you cover the hanky with the crayon.

33

Which is warm?

What kind of clothes do you wear in cold weather? Winter clothes are made from thick, soft materials, such as wool. These materials stop the warmth from escaping from your body. Even when it is freezing outside, you stay warm inside your clothes.

Now try this test
You will need: ★ 3 cups with lids ★ a pitcher of warm water ★ a fridge ★ a watch ★ rubber bands ★ cotton balls ★ aluminum foil

cotton balls

aluminum foil

1 Ask an adult to pour the same amount of warm water into three cups. Put the lids on.

rubber bands

2 Wrap one cup in cotton and one in foil. Hold the cotton and foil in place with rubber bands.

Keeping warm

This Inuit boy lives in Alaska where it is very cold all of the time. To keep warm, he wears clothes made of thick fur.

Science explained

Soft, thick materials, such as cotton balls, are best at keeping in warmth. Aluminum foil keeps some warmth in, but not as much as cotton balls. The water in the uncovered cup cools down fastest. It has no extra layer to trap the heat inside the cup.

Use a watch to time 10 minutes.

3 Leave the third cup uncovered. Put the cups in the fridge, and take them out after 10 minutes.

4 Test the water with your finger. Which cup feels the hottest? Which feels the coldest?

Amazing magnets

Have you ever dropped a pile of pins? It's easy to pick them up with a magnet. Some metal things, such as pins and paper clips, stick to magnets but others do not. Find out which materials can be picked up by amazing magnets.

Now go fishing

You will need: ★ colored construction paper ★ scissors ★ adhesive tape ★ aluminum foil ★ metal paper clips ★ used matchsticks ★ a ruler ★ a small magnet ★ a piece of string about 12 in (30 cm) long or thick, cotton thread

1 Ask an adult to help you cut the construction paper into nine fish shapes, each about 2 in (5 cm) long.

used matchstick

aluminum foil

metal paper clip

adhesive tape

2 Tape small pieces of foil to three of the fish. Tape paper clips to three more fish and matchsticks to the rest of the fish.

Mighty magnets

This huge magnet is strong enough to pick up heavy pieces of metal in a scrap yard.

Hold your fishing pole over the fish.

3 Tape a piece of string to one end of the ruler, and tie a magnet to the end of the string.

This is your fishing pole.

4 Now turn over all the fish so that you cannot see what is stuck onto them. Use your magnet fishing pole to try and catch the fish. How many can you catch?

When you have caught a fish, turn it over to see what is stuck to it.

It's quiz time!

Now that you have completed the experiments, have fun testing your knowledge about materials. Look back for help if you are unsure of any of the answers.

Let's go!

Can you find what doesn't belong?
Look at the lists of words below. Can you figure out which word in each line is unlike the others?

1   hard   soft   blue   rough

2   diamond   metal   soap   stone

3   brick   glass   plastic wrap   window

Can you choose the correct words?
Look at each sentence below. Choose which one of the three shaded words makes the sentence true.

How's it going?

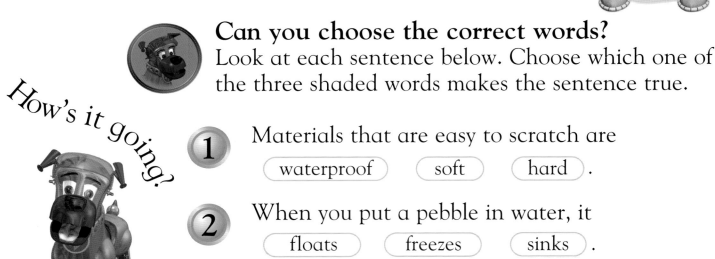

1   Materials that are easy to scratch are
(waterproof)   (soft)   (hard) .

2   When you put a pebble in water, it
(floats)   (freezes)   (sinks) .

3   When you bend dry spaghetti, it
(breaks)   (stretches)   (floats) .

What's going on?

Can you answer the questions below?

1 What happens to the boat-shaped piece of modeling clay when it is put in the water?

2 What is helping to keep Pixel and Chip dry?

3 Why is the magnet picking up Newton?

Now check your answers.

Give yourself one point for each correct answer.

What's going on?

1 The boat shape will float when it is put in the water, because its shape makes it light for its size.
2 The waterproof umbrella is helping keep Pixel and Chip dry.
3 The magnet is able to pick up Newton because Newton is made of steel, a metal that magnets attract.

Choose the correct words

1 Soft
2 Sinks
3 Breaks

What doesn't belong?

1 Blue – the other words describe the feel of materials.
2 Soap – the other materials are all hard.
3 Brick – the other things are completely see-through.

Using Materials

Parents' notes

Working through this section will help your child to discover why different materials are suitable for different purposes. Read these notes and any on the relevant pages to help your child get the most out of the experiments.

Pages 44–45: Sorting materials

This activity encourages your child to think about the differences between natural and manufactured materials. Explain that natural materials can be mixed together or treated with heat to make new, manufactured materials. For example, sand is melted to make glass.

Pages 46–47: Hard as stone

The fast-running tap water shows your child how stone can withstand the effect of rain, whereas other weaker or lighter materials may wash away. Discuss what happens in storms and floods – stone buildings get wet but usually remain standing. Houses made from mud or sticks may be washed away. You may want to plug the drain with a stopper.

Pages 48–49: Sandcastles

Adding the correct amount of water to make a sturdy sandcastle is tricky! Encourage your child to experiment with different amounts of water and to compare the results. The strength of each castle can be tested by gradually placing pebbles on top of it.

Pages 50–51: Wood is good

You will need to cut out the wood and to supervise your child closely when he or she is gluing. Explain why certain glues can be dangerous. Varnishing the toy furniture will waterproof the wood, making it harder wearing. After the activity, discuss with your child the advantages and disadvantages of making things out of wood; for example, it is easy to cut and shape, but it can catch on fire or rot.

Pages 52–53: Paper shapes

This activity shows your child that paper is a flexible material that is easy to fold into different shapes. Discuss how paper absorbs the ink from felt-tip pens but how too much liquid makes paper soggy.

Pages 54–55: Weaving yarn

Encourage your child to concentrate on going in and out with the needle, since it is easy to miss a line of the string. When he or she has completed a row, push the line of yarn up toward the previous row so that the weave is tight. Make sure your child is careful when using the darning needle.

Pages 56–57: Plastic parts

You will need to supervise the gluing. Point out that, unlike the previous materials, plastic is an artificial, or manufactured, material. Encourage your child to use other plastic objects for the model if you do not have all those listed. Afterward, suggest that he or she paints it.

Pages 58–59: Made of metal

Your child might need help identifying and collecting metal objects. Explain that there are many different types of metal. It may be appropriate for you to name them. Explain that different metals have different individual qualities. For example, aluminum foil is shiny and easy to fold, but keys are stiff and strong.

Pages 60–61: Clear as glass

Suggest to your child that he or she looks for examples of stained-glass windows, either in buildings or in books. This could inspire his or her design. However, make sure the design is not too complicated. Cutting with the utility knife will need to be done by an adult. Help your child place the colored plastic against a window so that he or she can see how light shines through it.

Pages 62–63: Building bricks

Mix the cement for your child to make sure that the quantities are correct for the brick to set. If the quantities of water and mixture recommended on the pack are different from those in the experiment, follow the pack's instructions. When the cement brick has set, encourage your child to test its durability by leaving it outside in the wind and rain.

Sorting materials

What is the difference between wood and plastic? Wood is a natural material, but plastic is made by people. Look at the things around you. Do you know which materials are natural and which are made?

Now make a collage picture

You will need: ★ a box of lots of different, small things, such as beads, stones, twigs, bottle tops, leaves, dried pasta ★ glue ★ a felt-tip pen ★ a piece of thick cardboard ★ a ruler

dried pasta

wire pipe cleaner

sunflower seeds

twig

bottle top

marble

plastic beads

shell

Draw the margin in felt-tip pen

pebble

leaf

1 Use a ruler to measure out a margin 2 in (5 cm) in from the edge of the piece of cardboard. Draw the margin all the way around the cardboard.

2 Look at the things in the box. What are they made of? Sort them into two groups – one for things that are natural and one for things that are not.

reed
thatch

mud
walls

wooden
poles

wooden
door

A natural house

In some parts of the world, people build houses with natural
materials they find around them. This African house is
made from sunbaked mud, wood, and dried grass called reed.

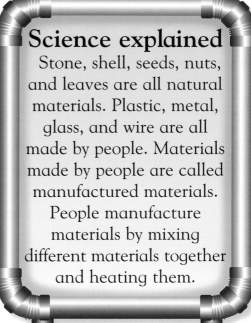

Science explained

Stone, shell, seeds, nuts,
and leaves are all natural
materials. Plastic, metal,
glass, and wire are all
made by people. Materials
made by people are called
manufactured materials.
People manufacture
materials by mixing
different materials together
and heating them.

3 Now glue the
things onto
the cardboard to
make a collage
picture. Glue all the
things made from
natural materials in
the center of the
picture and all the
other things in
the border.

Hard as stone

On a wet and windy day, which do you think would last longer – a house made out of twigs or a house made out of stone? Try this test to find out which is the most hard-wearing natural material.

Now try this test

You will need: ★ an old colander ★ a bucket ★ some sand ★ stones ★ some twigs ★ some soil ★ a stick ★ a tray

sand

bucket

⚠ Wash your hands after touching soil.

soil

stones

twigs

1 Pour the soil and sand into the bucket, then put the twigs and stones on top. Shake the bucket to mix everything together, or stir everything with a stick.

2 Place the colander on a tray. Pour everything in the bucket into the colander.

soil mixture

colander

tray

3 Hold the colander over a sink. Turn on a cold faucet, and let the water wash through the mixture for a few minutes.

water from the cold faucet

Sand and soil coming out with the water.

Lasting rocks
In many places in the world, you can see rocks standing high above ground level. These rocks have lasted for millions of years.

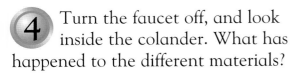

4 Turn the faucet off, and look inside the colander. What has happened to the different materials?

Science explained
When the faucet runs fast, the sand and soil run out through the holes in the colander. The twigs are washed away over the sides. Only the stones are left behind. Stone is the best natural material for building a strong house that will last, even in a severe storm.

Sandcastles

Sand is fun to play with. If you jump into it, you'll have a soft landing. But is it good for building things? Mix different amounts of sand and water to see which makes the best sandcastle.

Now make a sandcastle

You will need: ★ a bucket ★ some play sand ★ a spade ★ a large tray or sand tray ★ pebbles ★ some shells ★ a pitcher of water

Mix the sand and water with a spade.

Pour the sand over a sand tray, or do this experiment outside.

1 Fill the bucket with dry sand, and pat it down. Tip the bucket over to make a sandcastle. What happens? Have you made a sandcastle?

2 Fill the bucket with sand again, but this time add about a cupful of water to the sand. Mix the sand and water together with the spade, and pat it down firmly on top.

Sand sculpture

This amazing sculpture was made out of wet sand. The sculptor had to keep spraying the sand sculpture with water to keep it from drying out and crumbling away.

Science explained

Sand is made from tiny pieces of rock and shells, called sand grains. Mixing water with sand holds the grains together, making the sand stronger. A castle made with wet sand is stronger than one made with dry sand. If the sand is too wet, it won't keep its shape.

Decorate your castle with some shells.

3 Now turn the bucket over, and tap the base. Then lift it up gently to empty out the sandcastle. Is it firmer than the first sandcastle?

Put pebbles on the castle one at a time to test its strength.

4 Put some pebbles on the sandcastle. How many can you add before it starts to crumble? Make another castle with wetter sand. Is it stronger?

Wood is good

Wood comes from trees. It is a wonderful natural material because it grows. This means that as long as we replace the trees we cut down, we never need to run out of wood. Wood is used to make furniture, toys, fences, and many other things.

Now make wooden furniture

You will need: ★ a strip of balsa wood about 20 in (50 cm) by 2 in (6 cm) ★ a piece of sandpaper ★ nontoxic glue ★ kitchen scale weights ★ poster paints

Use the sandpaper to smooth down the cut edges of the wood.

balsa wood

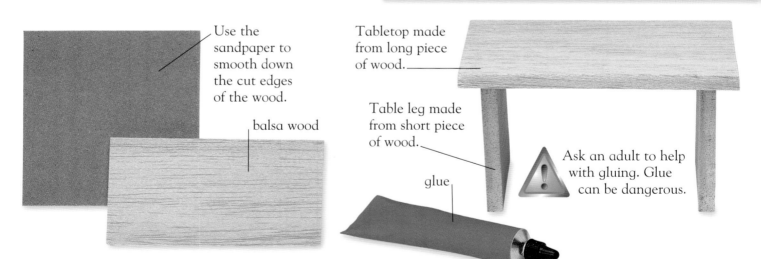

Tabletop made from long piece of wood.

Table leg made from short piece of wood.

glue

Ask an adult to help with gluing. Glue can be dangerous.

1 Ask an adult to cut the wood into two pieces measuring 5 in (12 cm) by 2 in (6 cm), and four pieces measuring 2 in (6 cm) by 2 in (6 cm).

2 Carefully glue two of the short pieces of wood to one of the long pieces of wood, as shown. Let the glue dry. You have now made a wooden table.

Science explained

Wood is a useful material for making things with because it is easy to cut, shape, and join together. It is light, but strong at the same time. Your table and chair can support a weight. It is easy to smooth out any rough edges on wood so that it looks and feels good, too.

Shaping wood

A carpenter uses all kinds of tools to make furniture from wood. He or she uses saws to cut it, chisels to shape it, drills to make holes in it, and planes to smooth it.

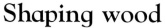

When the glue is dry, use the weights to test the chair's strength.

right angle from short pieces of wood

3 Glue the other two short pieces of wood together to make a right angle. Then glue them to the second long piece of wood as shown, to make a chair.

4 When the glue has dried, you can paint your table and chair in bright colors, like Chip and Newton are doing. For a shiny finish, cover the table in clear varnish, once the paint has dried.

Paper shapes

Writing paper, wrapping paper, tissue paper, newspaper – how many different kinds of paper can you collect? Think about all the things paper is used for, then try making something out of it yourself.

Now make a paper hat
You will need: ★ a sheet of paper about 17 in (42 cm) by 12 in (30 cm) ★ felt-tip pens ★ colored paper ★ scissors ★ nontoxic glue

1 Carefully fold your piece of paper in half, so that the two short sides touch. Crease it along the fold line.

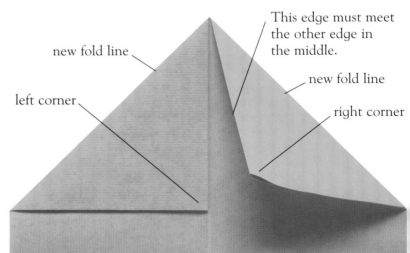

new fold line

This edge must meet the other edge in the middle.

new fold line

left corner

right corner

2 Turn the paper so that the fold line is at the top. Then turn down the top corners of the paper until they meet in the middle. Press firmly along the two new fold lines to make sharp edges.

It's party time!
Lots of things at a party are made of paper. There are paper hats and streamers, paper cups, and paper plates. Party invitations are made of paper, and presents are wrapped in it, too.

Fold this edge up first.

Cut some streamers out of colored paper.

3 Separate the two edges left at the bottom of the paper. Fold up the edge facing you, and crease along the fold. Then turn the hat over, and fold up the edge on the other side.

Be careful when using scissors.

Diamond shapes cut out of paper.

4 Put your hands inside the hat to open it up. Now it is ready to wear. You can decorate it by gluing on paper shapes and streamers, or by drawing on it with felt-tip pens.

Weaving yarn

Which material keeps you warm on a cold day? Woolen clothes keep you snug and cozy. Wool is a natural material that comes from sheep. See what happens when you weave threads of yarn together.

Now weave a mat

You will need: ★ differently colored balls of woolen yarn ★ a piece of cardboard about 5 in (12 cm) by 6 in (14 cm) ★ scissors ★ a darning needle ★ thin string ★ a pencil ★ a ruler ★ a hole puncher

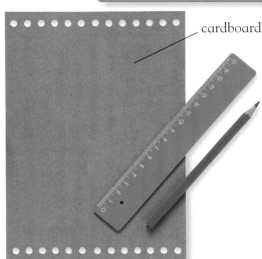

cardboard

Tie a knot around the cardboard at both ends.

hole puncher

thin string

1 Ask an adult to mark holes ½ in (1cm) apart along the top and bottom of the cardboard. Then punch the holes out using the hole puncher. This will be your loom.

2 Thread the string through the top left corner and tie a knot. Now thread it up and down between the holes, as shown. Finish at the bottom right corner and tie a knot.

Science explained

Your woolen mat is made from lots of threads of woolen yarn that you have woven together. If you look closely, you can see tiny holes between the threads in your mat. This means that although wool is warm, it is not waterproof.

Weaving at a loom

Weavers use looms to weave long threads of yarn into clothes or to make rugs and curtains for people's homes. Today, most wool is woven in factories using huge looms.

stripes of differently colored yarn

Tie each new piece of yarn onto the end of the last piece.

3 Ask an adult to thread a long piece of yarn onto the needle. Tie the yarn around the string in the top left corner. Weave the yarn in and out of the string, first one way, then back the other way. When you finish one piece of yarn, tie on another piece in a different color.

4 When you have finished the weaving, tie off any loose ends. Ask an adult to cut the cardboard carefully along the holes to remove the woven mat.

Plastic parts

Plastic is a manufactured material. We use plastic for all kinds of things, from thin, light shopping bags to tough cycle helmets. Try making a model out of pieces of plastic packaging that you can find around your home.

Now make a plastic pig
You will need: ★ 1 large and 1 small food tub ★ 2 plastic spoons ★ a bendy straw ★ 1 large and 4 small, plastic tubs ★ 2 buttons ★ glue ★ a plastic belt buckle ★ scissors

Ask for adult help with gluing. Glue can be dangerous.

glue

large food tub

small food tub

plastic buckle for nostrils

Eye made from a plastic button.

Ear made from a plastic spoon.

1 Use the large food tub for the pig's face. Glue on a smaller food tub for the pig's snout. Now glue on the buckle to make the pig's nose.

2 Glue on two buttons to make the pig's eyes. Then glue two spoons to the back of the pig's face to make the pig's ears. You have now finished the face.

Plastic toys

How many plastic things do you have in your house? Lots of toys are made out of plastic because it is easy to mold into different fun shapes.

large bottle

plastic tubs

plastic straw

3 Ask an adult to cut off the bottom of a plastic bottle. Use this for the pig's body. Glue on four plastic tubs to make the legs.

4 Now glue the pig's head to the open end of the bottle body. Make sure that the ears are at the top. Glue a drinking straw to the other end of the bottle to make the pig's tail.

Made of metal

Lots of everyday things are made of metal. You can usually tell if something is made of metal because it feels heavy and cold. Metals are often shiny, too. Look around for different metal things around your home.

Cut out one page for each of the objects you have chosen.

Now make a metal scrapbook
You will need: ★ different metal objects ★ scissors ★ a large piece of thin cardboard ★ a ruler ★ a pencil ★ a hole puncher ★ a paper fastener ★ aluminum foil ★ a marker

Be careful when using scissors.

Draw a picture here.

Write the name of your object here.

Key

pencil

scissors

ruler

key

1 Collect some metal objects from around the house. With a ruler and pencil, draw pages about 8 in (21 cm) by 4 in (11 cm) on the cardboard. Cut out the pages.

2 Draw a line down the middle of each page. On one side of the line, draw a picture of one of the objects, and on the other side, write its name.

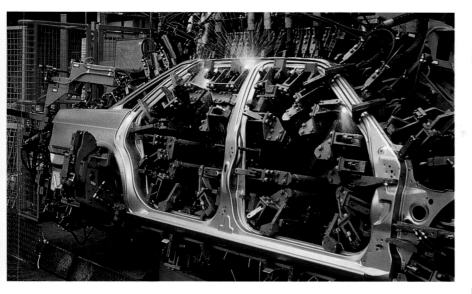

Making cars

The outside of a car is made from thin sheets of metal. In a car factory, robots join the pieces of metal together.

3 Underneath the object's name, list the reasons why the object is made of metal. Then make a cover for your scrapbook out of aluminum foil. Ask an adult to make a hole with the hole puncher at the top of each page, including the cover.

My Book of Metal Objects

Use a marker to write the title of your book on the cover.

Punch a hole in each page here.

Key

- It is strong – it won't bend.
- It is durable.
- It can be made into different shapes.

4 Fasten the cover and pages of the book together with a paper fastener.

Clear as glass

Do you know why glass is used to make windows? The answer is because we can see through it. Some plastic is see-through, too. It is safer than glass because it does not shatter into sharp pieces. Both glass and plastic are manufactured materials.

Now make a plastic window

You will need: ★ see-through plastic in different colors or some colored candy wrappers ★ a piece of cardboard ★ a ruler ★ adhesive tape ★ a utility knife ★ a pencil ★ double-sided tape ★ scissors

Stained-glass window

This stained-glass window is made of thousands of pieces of colored glass. Each piece of glass is held in place by strips of a metal called lead. The colors show up as the light shines through the glass.

1 Draw a design for your window on the cardboard. Ask an adult to cut out the shapes in the window with a utility knife.

double-sided adhesive tape

Turn your window over so that you cannot see the adhesive tape.

strip of double-sided tape

2 Ask an adult to cut out pieces of colored plastic slightly larger than the holes in the window. Tape double-sided adhesive tape to the edges of the pieces of plastic, then stick them over the holes.

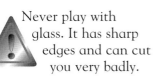

Never play with glass. It has sharp edges and can cut you very badly.

3 Ask an adult to help you tape the stained-plastic window to the inside of a glass window. Watch the light shine through it on a sunny day.

Building bricks

Bricks and cement feel just like stone. They are strong, hard, and rough to touch. Like stone, they are good for building walls and buildings. They are manufactured materials. Now make a cement brick; but watch out, it sets quickly!

Now make a cement brick

You will need: ★ a pitcher of water ★ a small bag of quick-setting sand-and-cement mortar ★ a small, plastic bucket ★ a spade ★ a plastic margarine tub ★ a wooden stick ★ a spoon

Never handle cement powder yourself. Always ask an adult to help you.

Add the water slowly, stirring all the time.

spade

wet cement

margarine tub

1 Ask an adult to fill one third of the bucket with the sand-and-cement mixture. Stir in just enough water to make a smooth, thick paste.

2 Use the spade to fill the margarine tub with the wet cement mixture. Fill it up to the narrow rim near the top.

Science explained

When the cement mixture has set, the brick is very hard. Your brick will even last outside in the wind and the rain. Cement is long lasting, so it makes a good building material. If cement is mixed with stone, sand, and water, it makes concrete, which is used to make bridges and walls.

Building a wall

This man is building a wall with concrete bricks. He is sticking them together with mortar. This is a mixture of sand and cement, the same as the mixture you used to make your brick.

Use a stick to draw a shape.

The brick keeps its shape when you take it out of the mold.

3 Smooth over the surface of the cement with the spade. Then wet the end of the stick and draw a shape in the cement.

4 Leave the brick for a few hours, until it has dried. Then turn the mold upsidedown and carefully tip the brick out. What happens if you leave your brick outside?

It's quiz time!

Now that you have completed the experiments, have fun testing your knowledge of different materials. Look back for help if you are unsure of any of the answers.

Let's go!

Can you find what doesn't belong?
Look at the lists of words below. Can you figure out which word in each line is unlike the others?

1 sand   soil   wood   plastic

2 brick   paper   cement   concrete

3 paper clip   brick   key   saucepan

Can you choose the correct words?
Look at each sentence below. Choose which one of the three shaded words makes the sentence true.

How's it going?

1 The best material to build a house with is
   (glass)   (stone)   (soil) .

2 Sandcastles can be washed away by the
   (sea)   (bucket)   (Sun) .

3 Wool is a natural material that comes from
   (wind)   (people)   (sheep) .

What's going on?
Can you answer the questions below?

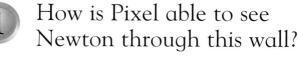

1 How is Pixel able to see Newton through this wall?

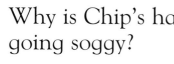

2 Why is Chip's hat going soggy?

3 How will the cement make it difficult for Newton to move his paws?

Now check your answers.

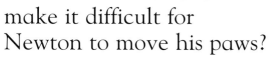

What's going on?

1 Pixel can see Newton because she is looking through a transparent glass window.

2 Chip's hat is soggy because it is made from paper and soaking up the rainwater.

3 It is difficult for Newton to move his paws because when water is added to cement powder, it hardens and sets very quickly.

Choose the correct words

1 Stone
2 Sea
3 Sheep

What doesn't belong?

1 Plastic – the others are all natural materials.

2 Paper – the other words describe materials that are used for building strong structures, such as walls.

3 Brick – the other words are objects that can be made from metal.

Give yourself one point for each correct answer.

Well done!
More than 3 points

Very good!!
More than 5 points

Brilliant!!!
More than 8 points

Changing Materials

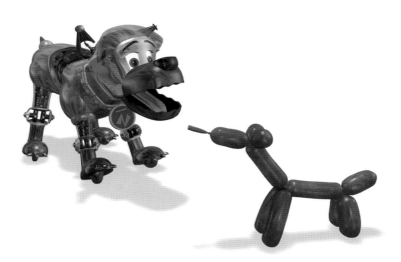

Parents' notes

Ice cream melts, toast burns, and gelatin sets. This section will help your child to discover how different materials change. Read these notes and any on the relevant pages to help your child get the most out of the experiments.

Pages 70–71: Changing shape

This activity shows your child how, for example, squashing and stretching change the shape of materials. Encourage your child to describe his or her own actions so that using words such as *twist, roll,* and *squash* becomes more familiar.

Pages 72–73: Print a shape

Your child will learn that some materials are soft enough to be molded by objects pressed into them. He or she could try out different objects or other interesting shapes for making a print, for example, a shell or a piece of bark.

Pages 74–75: Stretch it out

This activity demonstrates to your child that when some materials are stretched they stay at their new length, for example, modeling dough, while others spring back, such as rubber bands. Warn your child that rubber bands can snap if overstretched and may hurt someone.

Pages 76–77: Bend and twist

This fun balloon activity encourages your child to see how twisting and bending can completely alter an object's original shape. After making the balloon hat, he or she could experiment with twisting and bending paper shapes to decorate the hat. You might like to explain that bending creates curved shapes and twisting turns parts of the shape in opposite directions.

Pages 78–79: Melting

Making melted chocolate shapes is fun. Make sure that you heat up the water, pour it into the larger bowl, and place the smaller bowl in the water. The process of melting changes a solid into a liquid. After cooling, the liquid changes back into a solid again. This is known as a reversible change. Explain to your child that the newly set chocolate does not look exactly the same as the original solid chocolate bar, but it's still a solid.

Pages 80–81: Bake it hard

Making a clay pot introduces the idea of a permanent, or irreversible, change. The heat of the sun or a kiln turns the soft clay into a hard object. Once the clay is heated, it cannot change back to its original soft form.

Pages 82–83: Mix it together

Mixing and baking cookies provides another example of a permanent, or irreversible, change. The difference between the clay pot and cookies is that the cookies are made when several ingredients are combined, whereas the clay pot is produced from one substance.

Pages 84–85: Dissolve it

Dissolving is another way that materials mix with each other, and there are lots of everyday examples on these pages that will help your child to understand this. Explain that gelatin dissolves only in hot water and then sets as it cools. Sugar and salt are other examples of solids that can mix into, or dissolve in, liquids.

Pages 86–87: Let it set

When cold water is added to plaster powder, a chemical reaction begins. The mixture is liquid at first, but as the tiny grains mix and stick together, the liquid becomes a solid. This is another example of a permanent change.

Pages 88–89: Heat it

Using heat can alter the appearance and smell of some materials. Making secret invisible pictures or messages is a fun activity. Your child will see how heat produces a permanent change when it cooks the lemon juice. Make sure you do the ironing part of this activity for your child.

Changing shape

You can't squash a wooden pencil or bend a metal coin with your fingers. Wood and metal are too strong. But have you ever squashed a ball of clay or stretched a rubber band? Some materials change shape easily.

Now try this
You will need: ★ a sponge
★ a plastic cup ★ a plastic egg cup
★ a ball of modeling clay

plastic cup

Twist the sponge as much as you can.

1 First see if you can change the shape of the sponge. Can you stretch it, flatten it, twist it, squeeze it, and bend it? What happens when you let go?

2 Can you make the sponge smaller? It is bigger than the cup, but see if you can squash it inside.

Science explained

Sponge is a very springy material. It always springs back to its starting shape. Clay does not spring back. You can make the sponge smaller because it is full of holes. When you squeeze it, air comes out of the holes and they close up. The clay does not have air holes, so you can't make it smaller.

Rolling dough

A cook takes a ball of dough and rolls it out with a rolling pin. This changes it into a thin, flat shape, ready to be made into the crusts of tarts and pies.

How much can you twist the clay?

Squash and roll the clay into different shapes.

4 Chip is trying to squash a big piece of clay into a plastic egg cup. Can you make your clay smaller by squeezing it like this?

3 Now try the same experiments with the modeling clay. How does its shape change when you squash, squeeze, twist, bend, or roll it? What happens when you let go?

71

Print a shape

Have you ever followed a line of paw prints across a beach? When a dog walks on wet sand or soft mud, it leaves its footprints behind. You do, too! Mud and sand are soft materials. When you step in mud or sand, they mold, or fit, to the shape of your shoes.

Now make a leaf print
You will need: ★ a ball of modeling clay ★ a sheet of paper ★ a rolling pin or a plastic bottle ★ some leaves or twigs ★ some coins

You could try this with lots of differently shaped leaves.

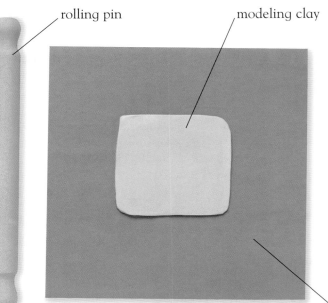

rolling pin

modeling clay

paper

1 Put a piece of modeling clay on the paper, and roll it flat with the rolling pin.

2 Put a leaf on top of the clay, and roll hard once more with the rolling pin.

Footprints on a beach

When you walk on a beach, the weight of your body pushes your feet down into the sand. Your feet leave prints behind.

Science explained

When you press a leaf or coin into the clay, the clay changes shape. It molds to the shape of the leaf or coin. But the picture left behind in the clay is reversed – like the image that you see when you look in a mirror.

4 Now try the same thing with a coin, like Chip is doing. Look at the print left behind. Is the picture the same as the one on the coin?

3 Lift the leaf by its stem, and carefully peel it off the clay. What do you see?

Stretch it out

When you stretch something, you pull on both ends to make it longer. Some materials stretch easily, but others tear or break if you try to stretch them.

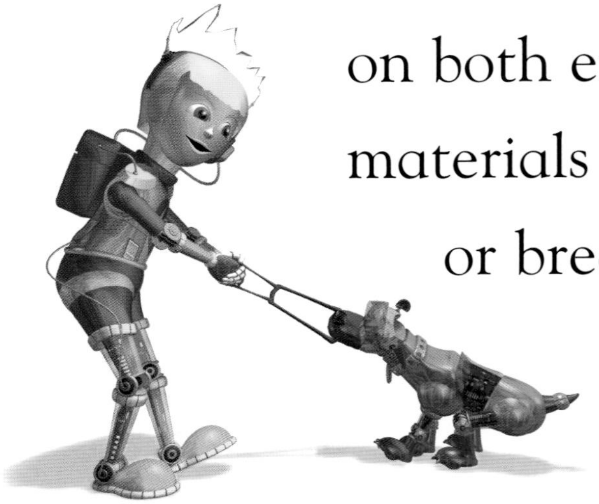

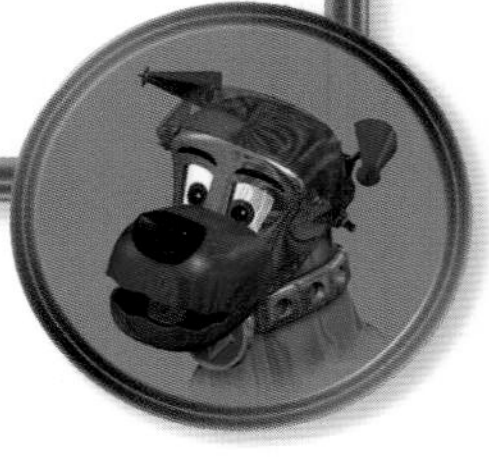

Materials	Does it stretch?	Does it spring back?
dough		
paper		
spoon		
rubber band		
plastic		

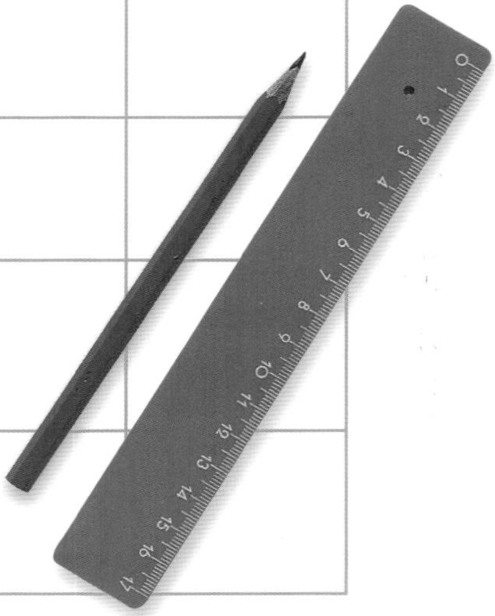

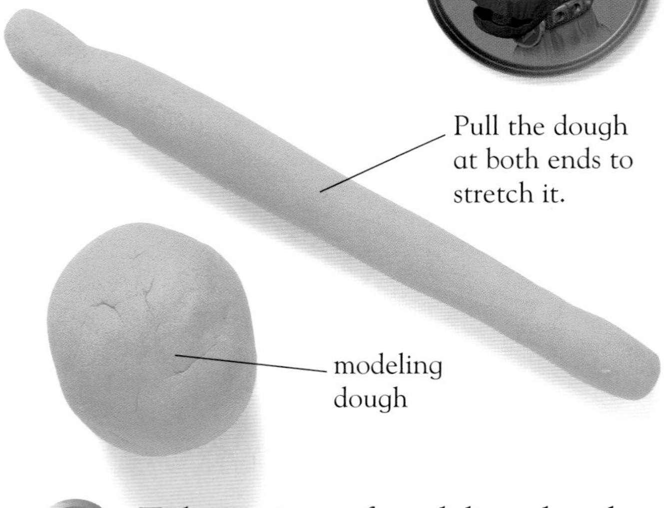

Pull the dough at both ends to stretch it.

modeling dough

1 Draw a chart like the one shown here. Decorate it with pictures of the materials you will be stretching.

2 Take a piece of modeling dough, hold one end in each hand, then pull. Does it stretch? If you let go, does it spring back to its starting length, or is it stretched permanently?

74

Science explained

Modeling dough stretches easily. It does not spring back to its starting length. Elastic and rubber try to spring back when you stretch it. Paper hardly stretches at all. It breaks if you pull hard. Soft plastic only stretches slightly. The plastic spoon does not stretch at all.

Materials	Does it stretch?	Does it spring back?
dough	✔	✘
paper		
spoon		
rubber band		
plastic		

Suspenders

This clown's suspenders are made from stretchy elastic. She can stretch the elastic to put the suspenders on, but when she lets go, they spring back.

strip of plastic

plastic spoon

piece of paper

rubber bands

3 Record the results of the experiment on your chart. Put a check or an X in each column.

4 Now try the test again with these other materials. Fill in the results on your chart. Which was the stretchiest material?

75

Bend and twist

When you bend something, you change its shape from straight to curved. When you twist something, you wind it into a corkscrew shape. How many times can you twist a strip of paper without tearing it?

balloon pump

Now make a balloon hat
You will need: ★ some long modeling balloons
★ a balloon pump

1 Ask an adult to blow up a modeling balloon with the pump and tie the end in a knot.

modeling balloon

Twist the balloon here and hold it.

Twist the balloon here and hold it.

2 Twist both the ends of the balloon to make them separate from the middle part.

Bendy straws

Bendy straws are useful for drinking from tall glasses. Can you see their special bendy parts?

3 Bend the balloon into a circle, then twist the two ends together to make a funny hat. Now try it on!

4 Can you make anything else by bending and twisting your balloons? Pixel has made an animal.

Twist the ends together here.

Melting

Have you ever eaten a bar of chocolate on a hot day? It melts in the sun and gets all over your fingers. Yuck! Popsicles melt when they warm up, too. The popsicle changes from solid to liquid and drips down the stick.

Now try this

You will need: ★ a bar of chocolate ★ a small bowl ★ a big bowl ★ hot water ★ a spoon ★ some small molds ★ a fridge

pieces of chocolate

Be very careful with the hot water.

hot water

The chocolate changes from a solid to a liquid.

1 Wash your hands. Break up the chocolate, and put the pieces in the small bowl.

2 Ask an adult to pour some hot water into the big bowl and put the small bowl in the water. Watch how the chocolate melts.

Science explained

Some materials melt when they are warmed up. This means that they change from being solid to being a runny liquid. The chocolate melts when you warm it in the hot water. Melting is a change that is reversible. When the chocolate cools down, it becomes solid again.

Melting candles

When you light a wax candle, the heat from the flame makes the wax start to melt. When you blow the candle out, the wax sets solid again.

A metal spoon warms up easily, so be careful.

chocolate shape

mold

3 When the chocolate has melted, it will be hot and runny. Use a warm spoon to pour it carefully into the molds.

4 Put the molds in the fridge until the chocolate has set hard, then take them out. To get the shapes out, turn the molds upside down and tap them.

Bake it hard

Clay is a type of smooth, sticky mud. When clay is wet, it is easy to mold into shapes. Potters make bowls, dishes, and jugs from wet clay. But a wet clay pot would be of no use – it would soon bend out of shape. So potters use heat to change the clay, making their pots hard and strong.

Now bake a pot
You will need: ★ an apron ★ some paper or newspaper ★ some potter's clay ★ a rolling pin or plastic bottle ★ a plastic cup

Try to keep all the stick shapes the same width.

paper

rolling pin

Press the cup down hard.

1 Put on an apron, and spread the paper on a table. Using your hands, roll some of the clay into several long, thin stick shapes.

2 Roll another piece of clay flat with the rolling pin. Turn the cup upside down, and press it into the clay so that it cuts out a circle.

Using a kiln

A potter bakes pots in a very hot oven, called a kiln. First she coats the pots with a special liquid, called a glaze, to make them waterproof. Then she puts the pots in the kiln until the clay and the glaze are hard.

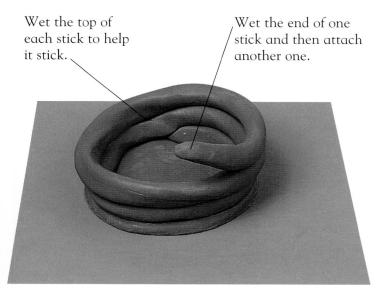

Wet the top of each stick to help it stick.

Wet the end of one stick and then attach another one.

3 Use the circle of clay as the base of your pot. Take one of the sticks of clay, and coil it around the edge of the base. Keep coiling it around to make the sides of the pot.

4 When your pot is finished, stand it in a warm, sunny place until the clay has dried out. This may take several days. Chip will have a long wait!

Mix it together

Some materials change when you mix them together. A cook makes cookies by mixing the right ingredients and baking the mixture in an oven. The heat changes the soft mixture into crisp cookies.

Now make some cookies

You will need: ★ 9 oz (250 g) plain flour ★ 4 oz (120 g) sugar ★ 4 oz (120 g) soft margarine ★ 1 teaspoon of baking powder ★ 1 teaspoon of ground ginger ★ some cool water ★ a greased baking tray ★ an oven ★ a spoon ★ a chopping board ★ a bowl

Mix the ingredients with a spoon.

baking powder

sugar

ground ginger

Make sure there are no big lumps left.

1 Wash your hands. Put the flour, sugar, ginger, and baking powder into the bowl, and mix them together.

2 Add the margarine, and rub it into the other ingredients with your fingers until the mixture looks like crumbs.

Papier-mâché

If you mix small pieces of paper and glue, you can make a new material called papier-mâché. You can make pots and jars out of papier-mâché.

Add enough water to make the mixture soft and smooth.

Sprinkle flour to stop the mixture from sticking to the board.

3 Add a little water, and use your hands to press the mixture into a ball. Then put the ball on a clean board.

4 Divide the ball into 16 pieces. Roll each piece into a small ball, and then press it flat on the baking tray.

⚠️ Do not touch the oven or the hot baking tray.

5 Ask an adult to bake your cookies in a hot oven (350° F or 180° C) for about 20 minutes, and then to take the tray out of the oven. Then leave the cookies to cool.

Dissolve it

If you stir sugar into a cup of tea or coffee, it seems to vanish. But it has really become part of the hot liquid, making it taste sweet. When a solid changes by becoming part of a liquid like this, we say that it has dissolved.

Now make a gelatin dessert

You will need: ★ a packet of powdered gelatin ★ a pot of hot water ★ a measuring cup ★ a plastic or wooden spoon ★ gelatin mold ★ a fridge ★ a plate

packet of powdered gelatin

Read the gelatin packet to find out how much water you need.

Stir the mixture to help the powder dissolve.

⚠ Be very careful with the hot water.

1 Ask an adult to boil the water and then measure out the correct amount of hot water in the measuring cup. Pour in the powdered gelatin.

2 Stir the mixture with the spoon. Watch how the gelatin dissolves in the water.

Salty sea

Do you know why seawater tastes salty? It's because it has lots of salt in it. You can't see the salt because it is dissolved in the seawater.

4 Place the mold in hot water for a minute, then tip your gelatin out onto a plate. Now see how it wobbles!

Place the mold upsidedown on the plate, then lift it up slowly.

Pour the liquid carefully, as it will still be hot.

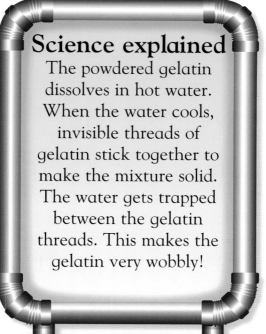

Fill the mold to just below the rim.

3 Pour the mixture into the gelatin mold. Put it in the fridge to cool and set.

Let it set

The bricks in a wall are stuck together with cement. When cement is first mixed, it is soft; but after a few hours, it sets hard. Some mixtures, such as cement and plaster, start as liquids but gradually change into hard solids.

Now make a plaster medallion

You will need: ★ a rolling pin ★ a plastic toy ★ a ball of modeling clay ★ a strip of cardboard ★ adhesive tape ★ a straw ★ scissors ★ plaster of Paris ★ an old pitcher ★ an old spoon ★ paints ★ ribbon

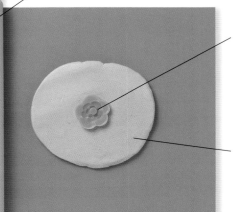

rolling pin

You can use any small plastic shape or toy.

The clay should be about $1/2$ in (1 cm) thick.

1 Roll out a piece of modeling clay about the size of your hand. Use the rolling pin to press the toy into the clay to make a print. Remove the toy.

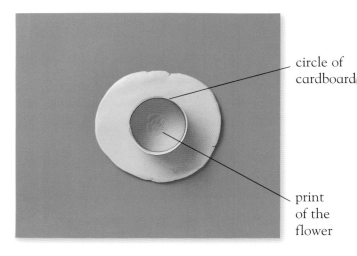

circle of cardboard

print of the flower

2 Bend the cardboard strip into a circle, and tape the ends together. Press the cardboard circle into the clay around the print.

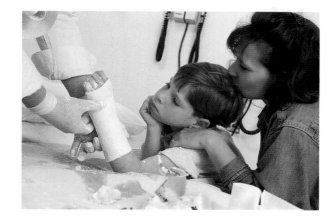

Arm in plaster

If you break a bone, a doctor may put a plaster cast on it to hold the bones in place. It goes on wet, but soon sets solid.

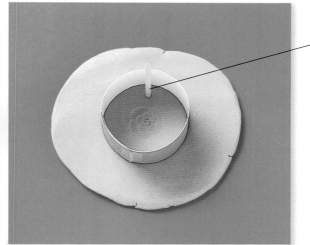

Put the straw near the top edge of your medallion.

Be careful when using scissors.

Paint the medallion with poster or acrylic paints.

ribbon

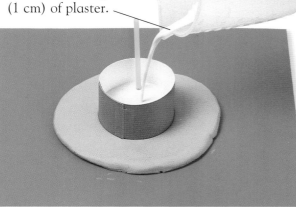

3 Cut off a short length of drinking straw, and press it into the clay. This will make the hole for the ribbon.

Pour in about ½ in (1 cm) of plaster.

4 Stir four parts of plaster with three parts of water in the pitcher. Pour the mixture into the mold, and leave it to set.

5 When the plaster has set hard, remove the clay, the cardboard, and the straw. Paint your medallion, and tie a ribbon through the hole.

Heat it

Do you like making and eating toast? Heat from the toaster cooks the bread, turning it brown. When you heat or cook food, you change its taste, smell, and color.

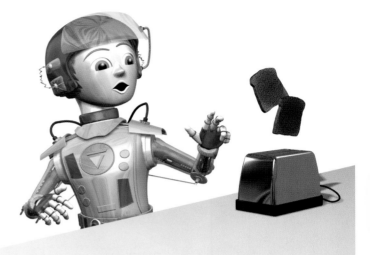

Now draw a secret picture
You will need: ★ some concentrated or fresh lemon juice ★ a small, plastic cup ★ a paintbrush ★ a sheet of thick paper ★ an iron

Drawing with charcoal
When sticks of wood are cooked in the middle of a hot fire, they change into dark charcoal. Charcoal is good for drawing. It makes black marks on paper.

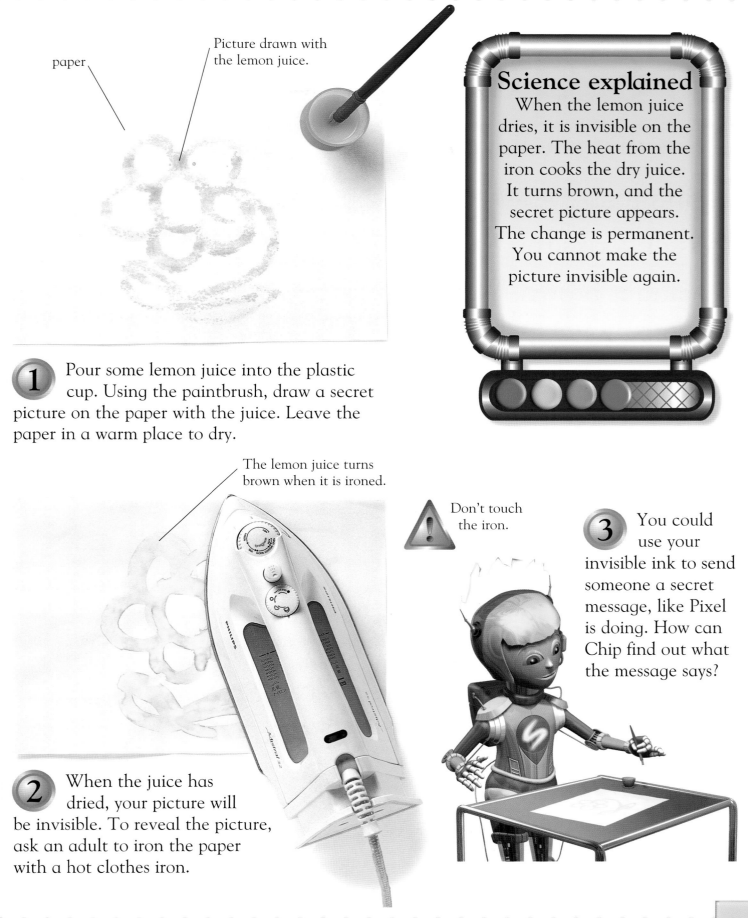

paper

Picture drawn with the lemon juice.

Science explained

When the lemon juice dries, it is invisible on the paper. The heat from the iron cooks the dry juice. It turns brown, and the secret picture appears. The change is permanent. You cannot make the picture invisible again.

1 Pour some lemon juice into the plastic cup. Using the paintbrush, draw a secret picture on the paper with the juice. Leave the paper in a warm place to dry.

The lemon juice turns brown when it is ironed.

Don't touch the iron.

3 You could use your invisible ink to send someone a secret message, like Pixel is doing. How can Chip find out what the message says?

2 When the juice has dried, your picture will be invisible. To reveal the picture, ask an adult to iron the paper with a hot clothes iron.

It's quiz time!

Now that you have completed the experiments, have fun testing your knowledge of how materials change. Look back for help if you are unsure of any of the answers.

Let's go!

Can you find what doesn't belong?
Look at the lists of words below. Can you figure out which word in each line is unlike the others?

1. bend   chocolate   twist   stretch

2. mix   bake   balloon   melt

3. brick   sugar   salt   powdered gelatin

Can you choose the correct words?
Look at each sentence below. Choose which one of the three shaded words makes the sentence true.

How's it going?

1. If you walk on soft mud, you leave behind
   (cakes)   (footprints)   (paper) .

2. On a hot day, chocolate
   (twists)   (melts)   (sets) .

3. When you bend something, it looks
   (curved)   (straight)   (wobbly) .

What's going on?
Can you answer the questions below?

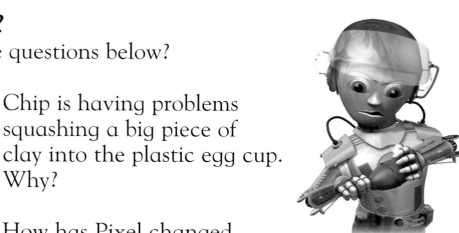

1 Chip is having problems squashing a big piece of clay into the plastic egg cup. Why?

2 How has Pixel changed this long balloon into a dog-shaped balloon?

3 Chip has put some pieces of bread in the toaster. What has happened to the bread?

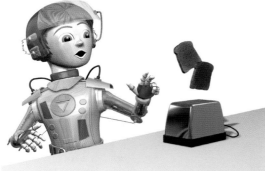

Now check your answers.

Give yourself one point for each correct answer.

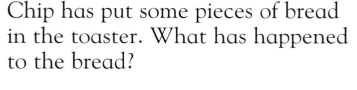

Well done! More than 3 points

Very good!! More than 5 points

Brilliant!!! More than 8 points

What doesn't belong?
1 Chocolate – the other words describe ways you can change a material's shape.
2 Balloon – all the other words describe processes that can change materials.
3 Brick – all the other words are materials that can dissolve in liquid.

Choose the correct words
1 Footprints
2 Melts
3 Curved

What's going on?
1 Chip is having problems squashing the clay because he can't make it smaller. This is because clay is solid and does not have air holes.
2 Pixel has bent and twisted the long balloon to make it look dog-shaped.
3 The heat from the toaster has cooked the bread and changed its color and taste.

Wonderful Water

Parents' notes

This section will help your child to develop his or her understanding of water as a liquid, as a solid, and as a gas. Read these notes and any on the relevant pages to help your child get the most out of the experiments.

Pages 96–97: Liquid water

These pages introduce three learning points to your child: water is a liquid, it flows, and it changes shape. To reinforce these points, your child could test other containers by transferring water from one to another.

Pages 98–99: Fair share

It's difficult for children to judge measures, especially if containers are different shapes. An "egg-cup full" is a manageable amount for a child to use as a small measure. When your child is confident, encourage him or her to experiment with bigger containers, such as cups and bowls.

Pages 100–101: Turning to ice

This fun activity demonstrates that when water is made very cold, it freezes to solid ice. To avoid confusion, reiterate the point to your child that fruit juice is mostly water. Make sure your child does not fill the ice molds right to the top, otherwise there will be no room for the water to expand when it's in the freezer.

Pages 102–103: Making steam

It's important that your child is aware of the dangers associated with fire, hot metal, and steam. Light the candle and hold the teaspoon over the flame for your child. Don't allow him or her to touch the steam. Encourage your child to observe and write down what happens to the water on the teaspoon and the mirror.

Pages 104–105: Drying out

To make this activity fair, all the hankerchiefs must be made of the same material, preferably cotton, and left to dry for the same amount of time. Depending on the climate where you live, you may need to vary the time the hankies are left – they should be left just long enough for the one on the clothesline to dry. If appropriate, explain that the hankerchief on the clothesline has dried because the water on it has evaporated into the air.

Pages 106–107: Water's skin

Your child may find it difficult to comprehend that water has a skin and how soap breaks its surface. It may help to explain to your child that this skin is very difficult to see because it's so thin. Reinforce the point to him or her that this skin is not like an animal's skin, but is the result of water drops on the surface holding together. Soap weakens the force between the water drops and breaks the skin.

Pages 108–109: Bubble fun

You might like to explain to your child that the outside of each bubble is a thin skin made up of water and dishwashing liquid. He or she will learn that no matter what the shape of the loop, the bubble that's blown from it will always be round.

Pages 110–111: Push it under

Here your child will discover that when an air-filled object, such as the ball used in step 1, is pushed under water, it will try to spring back to the surface because of the force of the water pushing it upward. If the air escapes from the object, for example the cup, then it will fill with water and sink.

Pages 112–113: Bubble diver

This experiment demonstrates that air is lighter than water. Encourage your child to explain to you that the pen top floats in the water because it has air trapped inside it. When the bottle is squeezed, more water goes inside the pen top, and the pen top sinks.

Pages 114–115: Amazing trick

Make sure that your child fills the cup right to the top and does the trick outside or over a sink. Discuss with your child how this trick works: the water's skin sticks to the cardboard holding it to the rim of the cup.

Liquid water

Splish, splash! Water pours, flows, spills, and splashes! Water is a liquid. This means that it does not have a fixed shape, like a solid stone does. Now see how easy it is to change the shape of water – but watch out – you may get wet!

See how the water takes the shape of the bottle.

Do this test over a sink or on a tray.

Now try this test

You will need: ★ a plastic pitcher filled with water ★ a sealable food bag ★ a plastic bucket or bowl ★ a plastic bottle ★ an empty dishwashing liquid bottle with top

Ask an adult to hold the bag open.

How many shapes can you squeeze the bag into?

1 Ask an adult to fill the pitcher with water and to pour it into the bottle.

2 Now slowly pour the water from the bottle into the food bag.

3 Seal the bag using the fastener. Gently squeeze the bag.

Science explained

When you pour water into a container, like a plastic bag, it takes the shape of that container. You can feel how water changes shape when you squeeze the bag. In addition to pouring water, you can also squirt it by squeezing the dishwashing liquid bottle.

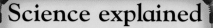

Water park fun!

It's fun going to a water park on a hot day. Cool water flows down the twisting slides and squirts out of jets. A wave machine in the pool makes everyone bob up and down.

First take the top off the bottle.

S q u e e z e !

4 Now fill up the pitcher again, then pour the water into the dishwashing liquid bottle.

5 Replace the top, leaving the lid open. What happens to the water when you squeeze the bottle over the bucket, like Chip is doing?

Fair share

If two cups are the same shape and size, they can hold the same amount of water. If the cups are different shapes, how do you tell how much water each one can hold? To find the answer, be a scientist and measure the amount of water in each cup.

Now try some measuring
You will need: ★ 3 differently shaped and sized plastic cups ★ a plastic pitcher filled with water ★ a pen ★ 3 adhesive labels ★ an egg cup

Keep filling the egg cup with water and emptying it into the cup, until the cup is full.

1 Line up three cups on a table in the order of how much water you think each will hold. Remember your guess.

2 Fill the egg cup with water from the pitcher, and empty it into one of the cups. Count how many egg cups of water it takes to fill the cup.

Science explained

An egg cup is a useful measure for a small amount of water. Each egg cup holds the same amount, so you can work out which cup holds the most water. In Pixel's test, the yellow cup held the most egg cups of water, even though it is not the tallest cup.

Different shapes and sizes

Which of these bottles holds the most liquid? It's hard to tell by just looking. This is because, like the cups in the test, these bottles are all different shapes and sizes.

Try not to get the labels wet, or they won't stick!

3 On a label, write the number of egg cups of water it takes to fill the cup. Stick the label on the cup.

4 Now test the other cups in turn, filling each one with egg cups of water. Write down the number of egg cups it takes to fill each cup. Which one holds the most water? Did you guess correctly?

Turning to ice

When it's very cold, water changes from a liquid into a solid, called ice. In winter, ponds freeze over and you might see icicles. But you don't need to wait for winter to see ice. You can make ice pops in the freezer!

Now make some ice pops

You will need: ★ a plastic pitcher filled with fruit juice ★ ice pop molds with sticks, or small plastic tubs and ice sticks ★ a felt-tip pen ★ a watch or a clock ★ a freezer

Make sure you don't fill the molds right to the top!

2 Using the felt-tip pen, mark a line on each mold showing the level of the juice.

level of juice

1 Ask an adult to help you pour fruit juice from the pitcher into each mold. Put the lids on.

Icy icicles

In the summer, water flows down this waterfall. But in the winter, when it gets very cold, some of the water freezes while it is falling. It turns into giant hanging icicles.

Science explained

Fruit juice is mostly water. Inside the freezer the water in the juice freezes into ice. The juice rises above the felt-tip pen mark because water gets bigger, or expands, as it freezes. When ice warms up, it turns back into liquid water again. This change is called melting.

3 Now ask an adult to put the molds into the freezer. Leave them for 3 to 4 hours.

If you don't eat your ice pop quickly, it will start to melt and drip down the stick! ———

4 Ask an adult to take the molds out of the freezer. Now compare the pen mark on each mold with the level of the juice. Has there been a change?

level of juice before freezing

5 Take an ice pop out of its mold. The juice has frozen into ice. The ice pop is now ready for you to eat!

Making steam

Have you ever noticed white clouds coming from the bathtub when it's being filled with hot water? This is some of the water that has changed into steam. In a hot bathroom, the mirror steams up so that you can't see your face!

Now try this experiment
You will need: ★ a candle in a holder ★ a metal teaspoon ★ cold water ★ a hand mirror with a plastic edge ★ a watch or clock with a second hand ★ a match

1 Ask an adult to light the candle. Put drops of cold water onto the teaspoon.

drops of water on the teaspoon

2 Ask an adult to hold the teaspoon of water over the flame.

⚠️ Do not play with matches or candles. Do not touch the flame, steam, or the hot metal of the teaspoon.

Steamy kitchen

Boiling food in pots and pans makes lots of steam, especially in a busy restaurant kitchen. The kitchen windows steam up so that you can't see out of them. The steam changes back into fine water drops when it touches the cold glass in the windows.

What happens to the water when it heats up?

3 Watch the water heating up. Use the watch to time how many seconds it takes for all the water to boil away.

Can you see the steam changing back into water?

4 Repeat the experiment, this time asking the adult to hold the hand mirror a few inches above the boiling water. What happens to the glass on the mirror?

Drying out

On a hot day, you don't need a towel to dry yourself after a swim. You quickly dry off in the sun! But where does the water go? It escapes into the air. The same thing happens to the water in your wet swimsuit when you hang it up on a clothesline to dry. Now do some laundry.

Now dry the washing
You will need: ★ 2 clothespins ★ string ★ 3 cotton hankerchiefs ★ a bowl filled with water ★ 2 trays ★ 2 chairs

wadded up hankerchief

1 Wet all the hankerchiefs in the water and wring them out. Put them on one tray.

2 Ask an adult to empty the bowl. Put one wadded up hankerchief back into the empty bowl

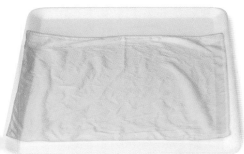

3 Spread out the second hankerchief on the other tray.

4 Ask an adult to string a clothesline between two chairs near an open window. Hang the third hankerchief on the line. Leave the hankerchiefs for one hour.

Put the tray from step 1 underneath the hankerchief to catch any drips.

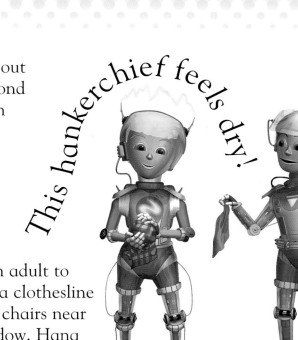

This hankerchief feels dry!

5 Now feel each hankerchief. Which one feels the driest? Which one feels the wettest?

Science explained

A breeze or strong wind carries water away into the air, so the hankerchief on the line dries first. The hankerchief on the tray takes longer to dry. The water can only escape from one side. It's even more difficult for the water to escape from the wadded up hankerchief.

Laundry-day weather

Have you ever seen laundry flapping around on a clothesline on a warm, breezy day? This is perfect laundry-day weather for drying wet clothes quickly.

Water's skin

Did you know that liquid water has a thin skin? The skin covers the top of the water, but it is see-through. This makes it very difficult to see. The skin is stretchy like elastic, but it is not very strong. Now try this experiment to see what happens when you weaken the water's skin.

Now make soap boats
You will need: ★ a bowl filled with water ★ a piece of colored construction paper ★ a drop of liquid soap ★ scissors ★ a ruler ★ a felt-tip pen

Follow the measurements shown to make your boats.

1 Ask an adult to draw two triangles on the sheet of construction paper and to help you to cut them out. These are now your boats.

← 2 in (5 cm) →

3 in (7 cm)

Be careful when using scissors.

A good scrub

This dog is having a bath because he is dirty. His owner is giving him a good scrubbing with soap and water. The soap weakens the water's skin, making it easier for the soap and water to get rid of the dirt.

Science explained

The water's skin pulls on all sides of the first boat, so the boat just drifts around. The soap drop weakens the water's skin behind the second boat. This lets the skin at the front of the boat pull it forward. The boat then shoots along quickly.

If you repeat this experiment, clean the bowl and refill it with fresh water.

2 Put one of the boats into the bowl of water. Does it move?

3 Place the second boat in the bowl. Squeeze a drop of liquid soap into the water behind it. What happens?

Bubble fun

Have you ever blown bubbles in the bathtub? Rub your hands together until they are really soapy, then make a soap skin in between your thumb and first finger. Now you can blow gently onto the soapy skin to make it into a bubble. Have fun, but be quick – the bubble will soon pop!

Now make some bubbles

You will need: ★ some dishwashing liquid ★ a tablespoon ★ a plastic cup half-filled with water ★ some pipe cleaners

Stir the mixture with the spoon.

1 Ask an adult to help you measure three tablespoons of dishwashing liquid into half a cup of water. Mix it well.

2 With an adult's help, make a loop in one of the pipe cleaners, like this.

3 Dip the loop into the soapy mixture.

Science explained

A bubble is a ball of air inside a thin skin of soapy water. The mixture of soap and water makes a stretchy skin that you can blow into a round bubble. Bubbles are always perfect balls, or spheres, whatever the shape of the loop you use.

Blowing bubbles

Bubbles are fun! It takes practice to blow a big bubble. The longest bubble ever made was 105 ft (32 meters) in length. That's longer than two buses parked end to end!

4 Now blow gently onto the mixture's skin on the loop. How many bubbles can you make?

Look at this one!

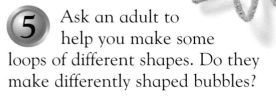

5 Ask an adult to help you make some loops of different shapes. Do they make differently shaped bubbles?

Push it under

It's lots of fun to play with beach balls at the beach or in a wading pool. You blow them up so that they are full of air, then they float on the water. Have you ever tried to hold a beach ball when it's under the water? It springs back up to the top!

Push!

Floating around

When you are learning to swim, you can splash around a pool in a plastic ring and armbands. The air inside the ring and armbands helps you to float in the water.

Now try these tests

You will need: ★ a bowl filled with water ★ a hollow, plastic ball, such as a table tennis ball ★ a clear cup ★ a spoon

Do these tests over a sink or on a tray.

Science explained

When you push the ball down and let go, the water pushes it back up. You can feel the water pushing back when you push the cup down, too. When you tilt the cup, a big bubble of air escapes from inside. The cup fills up with water and sinks more easily.

1 Hold the ball under the water with the spoon. Can you feel the water pushing back up? What happens when you let go?

Look through the side of the cup to see if there's any water inside.

2 Now hold the cup upside down and push it into the water. Can you push it under without getting any water inside it?

Look carefully at the inside of the cup.

3 What happens if you tilt the cup when it is under the water? Does the cup sink or float?

Bubble diver

Which way do the bubbles in a carbonated drink go – up or down? The answer is they always go up. The bubbles are balls of gas, like air. They always rise to the top of the drink because the gas is lighter than water.

Now make a bubble diver

You will need: ★ a clear, plastic bottle with a lid ★ a plastic pitcher filled with water ★ a clear glass filled with water ★ a plastic pen top ★ a small ball of modeling clay

The bottle should be full to the brim.

1 Press the ball of modeling clay onto the base of the pen top.

The pen top is your diver.

2 Put the diver in the glass. If the diver sinks, remove some of the clay to make the diver float upright.

Do this experiment over a sink or on a tray.

3 Drop the diver inside a bottle. Ask an adult to help you fill the bottle with water.

Make sure the lid is on tightly.

Deep-sea diving

Divers need to breathe in air when they are swimming underwater. The tanks on their backs are filled with air for them to breathe. When the divers breathe out, you can see air bubbles rising to the top of the water.

4 Screw on the lid. Gently squeeze the bottle with both hands and watch the diver dive. Now let go of the bottle. What happens?

 Never use a glass bottle for this experiment. It might break.

Science explained

When you drop the diver into the bottle, a bubble of air is trapped inside the pen top. The air bubble makes the diver light enough to float. When you squeeze the bottle, the water squashes the air bubble and makes it smaller. Now there is more water inside the diver. It is heavier, so it sinks.

Amazing trick

Do you think you can turn a cup of water upside down without spilling a drop? You can find out how to do this amazing trick here, but don't do it in front of an audience until you have practiced it first – then you can amaze your friends. Always do the trick over a sink or outside – just in case!

Now do an amazing trick
You will need: ★ a plastic cup filled with water ★ a piece of cardboard about 6 in (15 cm) by 4 in (10 cm) ★ a ruler ★ a friend to watch

The cup should be filled to the brim with water.

1 Fill the cup with water and place the piece of cardboard on the top.

2 Firmly hold the cardboard in place with the ruler, while you carefully turn the cup upside down.

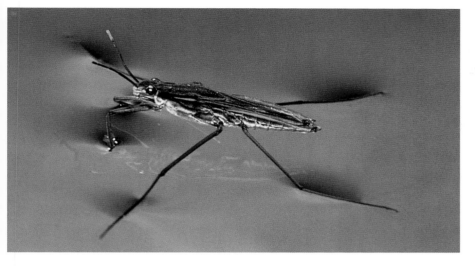

Water strider

This insect is called a water strider. It does an amazing trick! It can walk across water. Because it is so light, it doesn't break the water's surface. Can you see the dents that the water strider is making in the water's skin?

Science explained

The skin on the water pulls on the cardboard, holding it onto the edge of the cup. This stops air from getting inside. Because air can't get into the cup, water can't get out. But if you let some air in by gently pushing down on a corner of the cardboard, all the water will pour out!

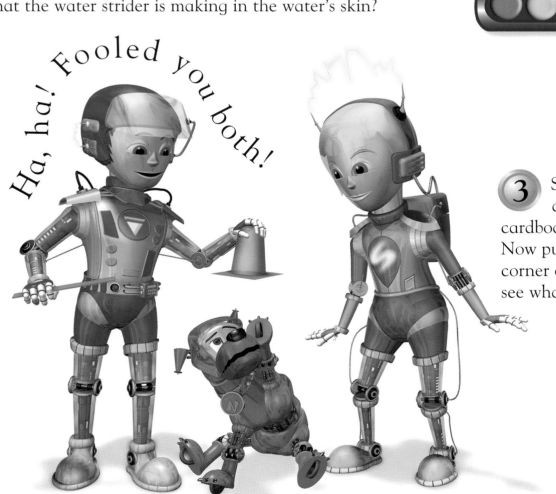

Ha, ha! Fooled you both!

3 Slowly slide the ruler away from the cardboard. What happens? Now push down on one corner of the cardboard and see what happens.

It's quiz time!

Now that you have completed the experiments, have fun testing your knowledge of water. Look back for help if you are unsure of any of the answers.

Let's go!

Can you find what doesn't belong?
Look at the lists of words below. Can you figure out which word in each line is not like the others?

1. ice   steam   chocolate   tap water

2. ice pop   bathwater   icicle   ice

3. melting   freezing   boiling   blowing

How's it going?

Can you choose the correct words?
Look at each sentence below. Choose which one of the three shaded words makes the sentence true.

1. Some of the hot water in a saucepan, kettle, or bath changes into (soap)   (steam)   (ice).

2. When you put liquid water in a freezer, it turns into (bubbles)   (ice)   (air).

3. Wearing armbands in a swimming pool helps you to (float)   (melt)   (sink).

What's going on?
Can you solve the questions below?

1 Pixel has just run a bath. Why can't she see herself in the mirror?

2 This hankerchief was soaked in water one hour ago. Why is it still wet?

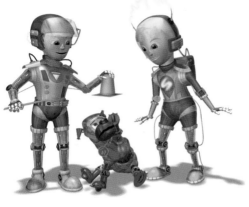

3 Why hasn't the water poured out of the upside-down cup?

Now check your answers.

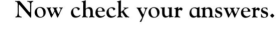

Give yourself one point for each correct answer.

Well done!
More than **3 points**

Very good!!
More than **5 points**

Brilliant!!!
More than **8 points**

What's going on?
1 Hot water from the bath has made the mirror steam up.
2 The hankerchief is balled up, so it will take a long time for water to escape and for the handkerchief to dry out.
3 The water's skin pulls on the cardboard, holding it onto the edge of the cup.

Choose the correct words
1 Steam
2 Ice
3 Float

What doesn't belong?
1 Chocolate – the other words are all forms of water.
2 Bathwater – all the others are examples of frozen water.
3 Blowing – the other words describe how water changes.

Glossary

Air

Air is the gas that is all around us. You need to breathe air to live. You can't see air, but you can feel it when it blows against your face or body.

Bend

When you bend something, you change its shape from straight to curved.

Boil

This happens when a liquid is heated to the point when it changes into a gas. When water boils, you can see bubbles of steam rising up and escaping into the air. Steam is a gas.

Bubble

A soap bubble is a ball of air that is trapped inside a skin of stretchy, soapy water.

Cement

Cement is a powder that sets hard when mixed with water. It is mixed with sand and stones to make mortar and concrete.

Dissolve

This is when a solid material mixes into a liquid. The solid breaks up and becomes part of the liquid.

Dull

Dull describes a material that doesn't reflect light well. Materials that are dull include pasta, wood, and leaves. Dull colors are the opposite of bright, shiny colors.

Expand

To expand means to get bigger. Water expands when it freezes into ice.

Float

To float is to stay on the top, or surface, of a liquid such as water. The opposite of floating is sinking.

Freeze

This happens when a liquid is cooled to the point when it changes into a solid. When water freezes, it changes into ice.

Gas

A gas is a substance, such as air, that spreads out, or expands, to fill all the space around it. Most gases are invisible.

Glass

Glass is a see-through material. It is used to make windows and bottles. Be careful when handling glass – if it breaks, its sharp edges could cut you.

Hard

Hard describes a material that is firm and difficult to scratch. Stone is a hard material. The opposite of hard is soft.

Hard-wearing

A hard-wearing material lasts for a long time, even in strong winds and storms. Hard-wearing materials, such as stone, are often used in buildings.

Heat

When you heat a material you make it hot. Heating can make a mixture harder; for example, a cake mixture gets harder when it is baked. Heating can also make a solid material melt; for example, a candle melts when it is lit.

Hollow

An object that is hollow is empty, or has a space inside it. Examples of hollow objects are boats, boxes, and balloons.

Ice

Ice is water that has frozen into a solid. In winter, when the weather gets very cold, water that drips off the roofs of buildings or from trees will sometimes freeze into icicles.

Invisible

When something is invisible, it is hidden and cannot be seen. For example, if you write a message or draw a picture using lemon juice, the juice is invisible until it has been heated.

Liquid

A liquid is a runny substance, such as tap water, that flows and takes the shape of the container that it is poured into. Cooking oil, shampoo, and orange juice are all examples of liquids.

Magnet

A magnet pulls toward it, or attracts, other objects that are made from some types of metals, such as iron or steel. A magnet does not attract other metals, such as aluminum.

Manufactured

Manufactured means that a material has been made by mixing or heating materials. Plastic is an example of a manufactured material. Manufactured is the opposite of natural.

Material

A material is a substance. Different types of materials have different features, or properties. Some materials can change their shape or form; for example, when some materials are mixed together, or heated up, a new material is made.

Measure

When you measure something you use a measurement, such as a cupful or the inches on a ruler, to find out how much of it you have.

Melt

This is when a solid material, such as ice, is heated up to the point when it changes from a solid into a liquid. An example of a solid material changing into a liquid is a bar of chocolate melting on a hot day.

Metals

Metals are a group of materials. Metals are shiny and strong. Most metals feel heavy and cold to the touch. There are many types of metals. Copper, iron, and tin are all examples of metals.

Mix

To mix is to stir two or more materials together to make a mixture.

Mold

When you mold a material, you change its shape. A potter can mold soft clay into the shape of pots and cups. Soft mud molds to the shape of your shoe.

Natural

Natural means something that is produced by nature. Wood and stone are examples of natural materials. Natural is the opposite of manufactured.

Paper

Paper is a thin, flexible material made out of mashed-up wood. It is easy to cut, fold, and shape, but isn't waterproof.

Permanent

Permanent means fixed. A permanent change to a material cannot be undone. For example, if you bake a cake, you cannot change the ingredients back to their original shape or form.

Plastic

Plastic is a manufactured material made out of oil and other materials. It is easily molded into different shapes. Plastic is used to make toys and for packaging.

Reflect

This is when light shines back off objects, particularly those that are smooth or made of metal.

Reversible

Reversible means not fixed. A change to a material that is reversible can be undone. For example, if you stretch a rubber band, then let go, it will spring back to its original shape.

Roll

To move by turning around and around or over and over like a stone rolling down a hill or the wheels on a bicycle.

Rough

Rough describes a material that feels uneven to the touch. Sandpaper, gravel, and bark are all examples of rough materials. Rough is the opposite of smooth.

Sand

Sand is a natural material made from tiny grains of rock and shell. Sand can be found in deserts and on beaches. Sand can be mixed with cement and water. Sand is used to make mortar and concrete.

Scratch

When you scratch something you scrape its surface and leave a mark. Soft materials, such as soap, can be scratched more easily than hard materials, such as metal.

See-through

A material that lets light pass through it is see-through. Glass and plastic wrap are completely see-through, but other materials, such as cotton and paper, only let some light pass through them.

Set

When you mix together certain materials such as powdered gelatin with water, or cement powder with water, they gradually stick together and start changing from a liquid into a solid. This change is called setting.

Shiny

Shiny describes an object that reflects light well. Materials that are shiny include metals, some plastics, and glass. A shiny material sparkles and looks polished in the light. The opposite of shiny is dull.

Sink

To sink is to fall to the bottom of a liquid such as water. If you throw a stone into a pond, it will sink to the bottom. The opposite of sinking is floating.

Smooth

Smooth describes a material that feels even to the touch. Plastic, glass, and metal are all examples of smooth materials. Smooth is the opposite of rough.

Snap

When something snaps, it breaks because it is weak. Dry spaghetti and thin wood snap easily.

Soak up

This is when a material mops up a liquid. Materials that have tiny holes in them, such as sponges and paper towels, are better at soaking up liquids than materials with no holes.

Soft

Soft describes something that is squashy or easy to scratch. Candle wax is a soft material. The opposite of soft is hard.

Solid

A solid is a material that has a fixed shape. It is not runny like a liquid. Bricks, sticks, and balls of modeling clay are all examples of solid materials.

Squash

When you squash a material, you push or press it so that it changes shape. Modeling clay becomes flatter and wider when it is squashed.

Steam

Steam is a type of gas that rises from boiling water into the air. Steam is very dangerous and can burn you.

Stone

Stone or rock is the natural material from which most of our world is made. It is hard-wearing and is often used to make buildings.

Stretch

When you stretch a material, you pull it so that it becomes longer.
For example, a rubber band gets longer when it is stretched.

Strong

This means that it will not break, or fall down, easily. Bridges and buildings are made from strong materials such as concrete, stone, and metal.
The opposite of strong is weak.

Transparent

Transparent describes a material that is completely see-through. Glass is an example of a transparent material.

Twist

When you twist an object, you turn different parts in different directions. Bread or pastry dough can be twisted to make interesting shapes.

Water

Water is a substance with no taste, smell, or color. Water is a liquid, but it can be frozen into a solid (ice) or heated into a gas (steam).

Waterproof

A waterproof material does not allow water to go through it.
This means that whatever it covers remains dry.

Wool

Wool is a natural material that comes from sheep. Threads of wool can be woven to make woolen cloth.

Index

Bye-bye!

The 99th Sheep

Meryl Doney

Illustrated by Taffy Davies

Tyndale House Publishers, Inc.
Wheaton, Illinois

Jesus told two very famous stories to show just how much God loves us. One we call *The Lost Sheep*. The other is usually known as *The Prodigal Son*, but it is really about two sons. One took his share of his father's money and left home. The other stayed behind but was very jealous when his brother was welcomed back.

In this story, I have mixed the two together and told them from the sheep's point of view. Jesus' message is still the same: God loves each one of us.

M.D.

"Oh, my poor feet!" said Curley as he limped down the track toward the fold.

It had been a long, hot day on the hillsides outside Bethlehem, and every sheep was glad to see the gray stone walls of home.

"Don't shove!"

"You pushed."

"Ouch, my hoof!" cried the sheep as they all tried to crowd through the doorway at once.

"One, two, three…" The shepherd began his patient counting. "65, 66, 67…" His practiced eye picked out each sheep as it passed.

"96, 97, 98, 99..." heard Curley as he limped in, last.

"Wait a minute," said the shepherd. "98, 99....
Someone's missing."

"It's not me. I'm here," said Curley.

The shepherd turned to look back up the track.
Already the sun had dipped behind the hill. The
path was empty.

"Judah. Ben. Help me count again," he called to
his two sons. "Onetwothreefourfive ... 98, 99...?"

"It's Daisy!" said Curley.

"Baaaa. Trust Daisy," said another sheep.

"Always trouble," came several more bleats.

"It's Daisy, I think," said Judah.

The shepherd sighed.

"You know what to do, boys," he said to his sons.

He hitched his water bottle back onto his shoulder, took up his crooked stick, and wearily started up the path.

The sheep settled down to sleep.

"Move over, I haven't any room."

"You've heaps of room. You're too fat."

"No, I'm not."

"Mind my hoof, clumsy!"

Judah pulled his cloak around his shoulders
and settled himself in the gap in the wall, making
himself into a human door.

Ben set out for the village to ask for help.

When Ben arrived in the village, everyone was preparing for the evening meal. He went to a friend's house.

"Please, can you help us? One of our sheep is missing," he begged. "It's Daisy."

"Daisy!" everyone laughed. "Not again!"

Out on the mountainside, Daisy looked up from the clump of grass she was munching.

"That's funny," she thought. "Where is everyone?"

She scanned the empty path. The tips of the hills were glowing pink in the last rays of the setting sun. There was no sign of the flock, the boys, or the shepherd.

A moment later, the sun dropped behind the mountains and the world was dark.

"Baaa," Daisy bleated in alarm. "Where are you? Sheeepherd!"

Without stopping to think, she began to run uphill. The path narrowed into a track. Thorns scratched her legs. Suddenly the path disappeared altogether.

"Help!" she bleated as she fell head over heels.

"Ouch!" as the brambles caught her.

"Baaa!" as she landed on a narrow ledge.

"Heeeelp!" she wailed. But her voice echoed away down the valley in the darkness.

The night was just turning to gray morning when
Daisy heard a tiny sound. Was it a voice calling?

High above her, two vultures began circling
lazily. Vultures love young sheep to eat. Daisy froze
with fear.

Then she heard the sound again. It was nearer
this time. It was definitely a voice.

"Baaa," called Daisy, as loud as she possibly
could. "Baaaaaa!"

"There you are!" The shepherd's face, tired and hot, broke into a delighted smile as he peered over the cliff.

Swiftly he scrambled down to the ledge and began to pull back the thorns.

"Soon have you out of there, Daisy," he said as he worked.

Finally he lifted her up in his strong arms, slung her onto his shoulders, and began the long trek home.

Daisy closed her eyes. She was safe!

Back in the fold, the sheep were restless.

"It's not fair," moaned Curley. "All this fuss over Daisy. She's always dreaming and wandering off."

"Yes," said another sheep. "She's just greedy, if you ask me. Serves her right if she is lost!"

"Would you like to be alone and lost on the hillside at night?" asked a kindly old ewe.

Curley looked up at the sky. He could see two vultures circling in the distance. He shivered.

The sun was just coming up behind the fold when Curley heard the familiar whistle. The sheep, who had been huddled together dozing, stirred and looked up. Striding down the path came the shepherd. And there, on his shoulders, they could just see the small woolly outline of Daisy.

"I found her," the shepherd called to his sons.

"Is she okay?"

"Yes, she's fine. A bit scratched. She was caught in brambles."

The boys ran to meet their father. The shepherd grinned his happiness from ear to ear.

"Go and get your mother and the neighbors," he said as he set Daisy down gently in the fold. "We'll have a breakfast celebration."

The sheep were not so delighted to see Daisy.

"Stupid," said one as she limped forward. "Causing so much trouble."

"It's not fair," said Curley loudly. "All this fuss over Daisy. *We* have been here all the time. *We* did not get lost. But Daisy gets the party. Shepherd's favorite!"

There was a long silence. Finally the old ewe walked over to the miserable Daisy and licked her nose.

"He's a good shepherd," she said. "He cares for every one of us. It wouldn't matter if it was me, or you, or Curley. If we were lost, he'd come looking for us. That's just how he is."

What a celebration breakfast they had that morning! The shepherd's wife brought newly baked bread. The boys carried water bottles and wineskins. The neighbors added figs, cheese, and olives. And the shepherd played his pipes.

Daisy kept close to the shepherd. And so did Curley, the 99th sheep.

The shepherd bent down and patted them both on their woolly heads.

"There," he said gently. "This party is for everyone."